Stig Jørgensen

REASON AND REALITY

Acta Jutlandica LXII
Social Science Series 17

AARHUS UNIVERSITY PRESS
1986

Printed by KJ Offset, Odder
ISBN 87 7288 002 3
ISSN 0106 0937

AARHUS UNIVERSITY PRESS
Aarhus University
DK-8000 Århus C
Tel. 06 19 70 33

Published with the support of the Danish
Social Science Research Council and the
Gangsted Foundation.

Contents

Preface

The articles collected here under the title *Reason and Reality* (Grounds and Motives for Legal and other Decisions) have their dealing with the basic elements of our political, moral and legal decisions in common.

The analysis of these elements demonstrates that there is an essential relationship between the different types of decisions. The fact is that they are all the outcome of a mental process guided by purposes and motives. These purposes can be normative as well as pragmatic and thus refer to both legal and moral rules and changes in reality.

If decisions are not to be irrational but are to meet the *demand for reason*, there must be given grounds for these decisions in the form of arguments. There must be given grounds for the legal decision for the sake of legal security, which is another aspect of foreseeability and reliance, the preconditions of the existence of any organization or society. The same reasons make grounds imperative also for political and moral decisions.

Motive and ground are not identical phenomena but usually two aspects of the same token. The motive is the actual psychological *cause*, whereas the ground is the argument *justifying* the decision by referring to the norms or values which are considered to be valid by the parties.

Motive and ground are thus of different logical categories, but the decision must not necessarily be motivated by other grounds than those referred to. On the one hand it is important to be critical as regards the grounds given by oneself and by others, but on the other it is a condition of the functioning of an organization or a society that one can trust the grounds given by others.

Opinions and decisions are not objective. Neither are legal and other normative decisions, which according to the previous conception were conceived as the outcome of a deductive process, a *conclusion* from an abstract rule to a concrete case. The reason why the legal decision appears in this way is that in its final form it has *selected* and *interpreted* the legal material and *qualified* the factual conditions, which are disposed to a legal decision, in a linguistic form suitable for the interpreted rule.

5

In ordinary as well as in legal practice not only the norms but also the reality has to be interpreted. This interpretation is not unbiased but is made in accordance with the *hermeneutic* background for the perception of reality. Our world picture, physical as well as ideological, helps us to see what we expect to see, and in a way also what we wish to see, so that we can *understand* our experiences. The legal ideology limits the regards which may be taken into consideration in the legal decision-making, whereas there are different degrees of freedom in the moral, political and private decision-making.

The *reality principle* demands that we respect the world picture and the natural laws which at the present time give us the optimal predictability of the real phenomena. The auditories, to which the legal, the political, the moral, the esthetic, etc. decision-maker addresses himself, are different with different ideologies. Therefore the arguments will also be different and thus not *objective*, but represent different degrees of *intersubjectivity* according to the extent, to which the addressees share the ideology, be it *professional* such as in legal, scientific and technical matters, or *political* in the widest sense.

Some of the articles deal with legal and moral decisions, others with the interrelation between socio-economic organization of society and legal-political rules. In particular some of the later articles analyse the possibility of the survival of *democracy* on the background of the analysis of the development and function of *contract and property right*.

The articles appear in English, although some were originally published in Danish.

Unfortunately Danish is no world language!

Stig Jørgensen

On Meaning, Opinion and Argumentation

What is the meaning?[1]

What is the meaning of stating that $2 \times 2 = 4$ or that the moon is made of green cheese?

What is the meaning of life?

I mean that the introduction of nuclear power is a crime against mankind!

What is the meaning of using the word or the term »meaning«: the meaning of »meaning«?

It is common knowledge that the reasons for disagreement more often have to be found in the circumstance that we are talking about different things than that we have different opinions of what is fact or what is a proper act.

All - or most - university graduates have been affected by the so-called »positivism debate« of the last decade.[2] The criticism of positivism has been based on the concept of meaning of the logic-empirical theory. According to this theory it has only sense to make statements, as the meaning of a sentence is identical with its conditions of truth, i.e. the criteria, which have been established in advance either in definitions or in accordance with a measuring tool.

Only such analytic or synthetic sentences referring either to logic-mathematically deductive systems or to measurable sides of reality can have meaning, as they can be either true or false. On the other hand metaphysical or evaluating statements are »meaningless«, as they have no »truth conditions« or criterias of truth.

According to this conception sentences as: »God is our creator« or »It is evil and unjust to preserve Capitalism« are without »semantic reference« and thus also meaningless.

Already a long time before the criticism of positivism philosophers had realized that it had sense to speak of pixies and mermaids, even though they existed only in the human imagination. Therefore, it is not meaningless either to speak of God and Devil, as most people understand the function of such sentences as illustrations of psychological and religious conceptions of human beings. In the same way it is possible to make statistical examinations of the views of Danes on what is good and bad, on the different political ideologies and other evaluations.

Since the philosophers David Hume and Immanuel Kant at the end of the 17th century introduced their cognitive criticism, it has, on the other hand, been generally accepted that there is a fundamental difference between cognition and evaluation, between »sein« and »sollen«, as it is in German.[3]

Theoretical cognition deals with the structure of reality, and it must therefore be subjected to the law of necessity, i.e. the law of causation; if not, it would be impossible to obtain and make a conception of reality. On the other hand our acts must be based on the condition of »freedom of the will«, for in case our will was not free, there was no basis for making us responsible, and without responsibility an organized social life among human beings is unthinkable.

The question is now, if the fundamental distinction between theoretical and practical cognition also means that there is no practical possibility at all of bridging between theoretical cognition and practical action. The outlook would be dark, if there was no difference at all between »rational« and »irrational« evaluations and actions. Common sense, which is a good foolproof against frantic consequences of logical systems, tells us that there are or ought to be possibilities of acting sensibly. Of course there are such possibilities, and in reality no sensible human being has ever denied that.

In this connection I usually tell the anecdote about the fameous surgeon who during a party authoritatively maintained that as he had now operated for so many years without ever encountering the soul, his common sense told him that there was no soul, to which the innocent one of the party - a lady I think - remarked whether he had ever encountered the common sense.

The curious thing about the criticism of positivism as it was at the end of the 1960s is, however, that it chose to throw out the baby with the bath water. The realization of the fact that cognition and evaluation were not two incompatible concepts led some people to believe in the irrationality of cognition, instead of aiming at rationality in evaluation and decision. As it had to be recognized that our description of reality cannot be reduced to the results of the measuring tools of natural science, and as it had to be recognized that the description necessarily contains some abstract concepts expressing our interests and aims such as: automobile, table, negligence, terrorist and so on, it also had to be recognized that all description was evaluating: political, as it was called in an extremely extended meaning of this word.

As Friedrich Nietzsche in the last century could say, »God is dead, therefore everything is permitted«, our so-called Marxists could about 1970 conclude that as cognition is not objective, all subjectivism is permitted. When all cognition is

»political«, as it was claimed, there was an apparent argument for using the science in the service of politics, and this meant with an odd shifting of the problems that only one particular political ideology had the right to represent the scientific truth, but that society's political control of the system of education and research in general is a means of oppression and »Berufsverbot«.

These wrong - or at any rate unnecessary - conclusions of actually correct premisses are, I presume, as a rule expressions of an unconscious manipulation of one's own consciousness or the consciousness of others, ruled by inner needs or interests, but one cannot and ought not ignore that somebody deliberately exploits an ambiguous way of presenting the problems in order to serve political objects.

However, one has to realize that the conclusion to be drawn from the non-objective character of cognition, is rather an attempt to »objectify« cognition as far as possible by defining the criteria, on which the description is based. The evaluations are bridges in the same way, and therefore they are not objective or absolutely subjective either, but *intersubjective*, as far as the definition of the conditions and criteria, on which one acts or to which one attaches great importance on making evaluating statements, *partly* will be based on problable assumptions of the structure of reality (cognition), *partly* will attach the evaluation to more or less generally recognized aims and interests.

And here we at last return to the concept of »meaning«. Consequently the word »meaning« has, as we have already seen, a quite distinct meaning within the philosophical language attached to a certain scientific theory. But »meaning« may mean something else; it may mean that the speaker has had a certain *intention* with what he said or did. It may also refer to the fact that the speaker wants to express a certain philosophy of life in general, for instance the belief in God. But it may also well be that the speaker in very modest phrases will express a philosophy, an attitude, an evaluation in general: That is my »meaning« i.e. opinion about this matter![4]

Opinions can be conceptions of reality-phenomena: »In my opinion most people are actually against nuclear power!« or »The deleterious effects of windmills are much less than those of atomic power stations«. But more often they are expressive of a political, religious or cultural evaluation, i.e. a statement of what is the right or wrong act in the speaker's opinion.

The concept that can combine statements of »meanings« i.e. opinions in general is: belief. »I believe, it is dangerous to build an atomic power station«, and: »I believe that it will be best for human beings to live in a socialist society«, or: »I believe that it is unjust to maintain the inequality of society«.[5]

Now you are naturally free to believe or say what you like. But you can only demand to be taken seriously in a debate on facts and acts, if you are able to adduce some arguments in support of your belief. Once it was defensible to advocate the belief that the earth is flat as a pancake, or that the moon is made of green cheese. Nowadays people advocating such a belief would not be taken seriously in the general social debate. To take that kind of assertions seriously would conflict with our practical interests in the treatment of the earth and the moon.

However, history proves that a wrong theory does not necessarily mean that you do not benefit by your search. »Search, and you shall find«, the Holy Writ deeply says; but it does not say what you shall find. The fact that the alchemists acted on a wrong theory and tried to make gold did not prevent them from learning useful things, which in an improved theoretical form became the foundation of the science of chemistry. In the same way astronomy was based on a wrong astrologic theory about the relation between the laws of the Universe and the laws of society. And so on.

I am aware of the danger of these considerations. By means of this argumentation all kinds of dilettantism and political and religious arts of seduction can be defended. But nevertheless we must be aware of the fact that the cognition can only be extended, if we accept new theories and ways of presenting the problems. Thomas Kuhn has actually wanted to speak of paradigm revolutions.[6]

An abstract debate about conditions of society in general will not do. The ordinary population, which is not trained in abstract thinking and argumentation, can only be engaged in a political debate, if it has a concrete grounding. Nowadays with the development of electronic media, the formation of opinions with its good or bad qualities is attached to persons and cases.

It is good copy, because it can be photographed and dramatized, and therefore in the nature of the case it is nothing but pseudo-events. This possibility of »cultivation« of dramatic and thereby engaged elements in these pseudo-events was first seen and exploited by the students of psychology in Copenhagen who in 1968 »occupied« and »blocked« their institute, but naturally they were inspired by similar student actions in Berkeley, Berlin, and Paris.[7]

Since then this kind of awakening technique has been used by the students to a high degree. However, many social groups and professional and industrial bodies have turned to these extra-parliamentarian methods: fishermen, seamen, farmers, printers, drivers, and in particular academic and semi-academic groups not to mention foreign terrorists and hijackers.

The particular thing about these actions is not that they solve any problems, but that they point out the problems and stimulate the spectators, the readers or the participants to engage themselves, to form an *opinion* (»meaning«) of the problems in order that this affection of public opinion may later on result in a solution of the problems and in a political action in quite other fields.

If we therefore by an *opinion* understand a *conception of or a belief in* the existence of a certain state of facts, or that a certain course of action is the right one, we must consequently be willing to or able to give *grounds* for this conception or belief, that is if we want to be taken seriously as *rationally* thinking or acting individuals.

However, we must not forget that these grounds are often a product of our attitudes, needs and ideas, which are deeply rooted in our nature and culture and that our description of actual facts often has to be made not in certainty but with different degrees of probability. It is self-evident that these factors based on feelings and uncertainty set limits to the certitude of your arguments especially in circumstances which are important to the society and its organization. For what is eventually a human being? How is the nature af man? What are his natural and what are his cultural needs? What conception of man is the right one?[8]

Here the agreement ceases and here certainty has to give way to belief; here lies the root of all political thinking. Man is as a matter of fact at one time a biological being with needs and limitations, but he is also able to adapt himself to the environments as well as he himself can make new environments, to which he can adapt himself. Man cannot hop on his tongue, but today it is impossible to say much definite about the nature of man.

However, things concerning the duplicity of individual/society, intellect/feeling, freedom/security, man/woman can be outlined without stating certain limits. And development-psychologists, sociologists and other professionals can no doubt speak about circumstances in the conditions of the individual and of the society, which result in an unfortunate or morbid development of individuals and society, but that is all together very uncertain.

But there are consequently many variations of opinions and therefore also a basis for different political conceptions of the »right« organization of society and the »good life« for the individuals. Therefore, there will always be a constant political struggle going on concerning the organization of society and the distribution of the social values. Here the demand for freedom and equality pulls in each direction, also because certain trades and interests make the social groups give different priority to these needs. It is self-evident that employers give a high priority to freedom, whereas the employees and those who qualify themselves for public offices will give equality the higher priority; the latter group because the carrying through of equality among different people will require a public bureaucracy and a welfare-system.

When all this has been said, it is quite understandable that the social debate may assume forms which do not harmonize with the ideal picture of the formation of opinions as being well-founded conceptions of reality or the right act seen in relation to a certain purpose.

A recently published investigation of modern »grass root movements« refers to the complexity of the modern society[9] as an explanation of the decreasing party-political interest. Not to be confused with the increasing political interest, which is reflected in the heavy polls. Besides according to the investigation the different interest groups have been integrated into the political system to such a degree that the traditional constituency organizations have lost their function of canalizing the political interests. Therefore, it is almost exclusively the material interests that influence the political debate.

On the other hand we could mention the political development in the struggle between »left« and »right« during the last century; also the development in the same period of the »folk high school« in opposition to the academic educational system could be mentioned here. The religious revivals have the same function as the people's revolt against the elite of society: landowners, officials, and ministers of religion. In the same way Christianity was once a proletarian movement, which used feelings and irrational arguments in the struggle against the existing system. At a later date Protestantism and Romanticism were similar irrational revolts of the lower classes against an existing rational elite society.

The development of Socialism towards reform Socialism which is a compromise with the established society is another example of the fact that the »irrational« people's opposition to the existing elite society has developed beyond the conditions, which were the basis of its »rationality«. Hegel/Marx made it quite clear that the organization of any society depends on the historical and material conditions, which demand structuralization, which again contributes to a new development which demand a new structuralization. The development of society will always move from a romantic-revolutionary phase, where new goals are laid down by feelings and needs, over an idealistic phase, where the efforts are concentrated on the carrying into effect of these goals and further on to a rationalistic phase, where the results obtained are administered, until the development of society passes its »rational« conditions, and enters upon a new romantic-revolutionary phase.[10]

At the moment we are presumably in an after-revolutionary phase, where new people's movements, which were aroused by the revolutions of the 1960s, try to mobilize the population on »idealistic« and »moral« demands to society. About 1970 the environmental problems took the rôle of the student revolt as the most important subject in the social debate. At the same time the catastrophism of the so-called »Rome Club« gave the starting signal to the ecological debate, which is concentrated especially on the idea of man's interdependence with nature and humanity in a global sense.

The »irrational« nature of these movements is reflected in their disconnected and incoherent argumentation in favour of their opinions and points of view. For instance the danger of explosion was the original argument against nuclear power stations in Denmark, later on it became the danger of terrorist attacks, etc., and nowadays the concern is concentrated on the risk by the radioactive waste. The inconsistence can for example be seen in the reluctance to compare the risk by nuclear power with the risk by alternative traditional energy supply. Similar examples can be found in the environmental and resource debate; among other things it is peculiar that the same groups demanding »zero growth« and retrenchments of the resources belong to the higher income groups and to the organs demanding higher income to their members.

I do not mention this because I want to initiate a debate on this basis. On the contrary it is my intention to show that this is impossible and also against the idea of the movements. I may seem frustrating to the expert, who thinks that he is to make an objective argumentation in favour of his well-founded opinions of technical and economic questions, to be disarmed by new arguments concerning quite different things.

As a matter of fact the intention is, however, to avoid to come to an agreement with the experts on these questions. On the contrary the intention is to throw suspicion on the experts by means of new questions and new assertions, which the experts may then go home and consider while the opponents are already preparing the next step.

As Bruno Bettleheim already wrote about the ideologists behind the youthful revolution:[11] Their intention is *not* to make people recognize their concretely formulated demands; if this were the case these knights of modern time would lose their »case« and have to go through an idle waiting for a new case. Therefore, the demands are constantly raised to such a degree that they can be quite sure that they (the demands) will not be fulfilled. By doing so they can secure the important group solidarity among the convinced and the appeal to cognated groups, which then identify themselves with the rebellion through the provoked group pressure of society.

Nowadays people talk about the »systemtranscendent« character of the people's movements. By compromising with the established society the public support is lost, Revisionism does not only betray the cause of revolution, it also takes the wind out of its own sails. That is what »Folkebevægelsen mod EF« (The People's Movement against the EEC) has learned, and that is what makes movements as OOA (organization against nuclear power) and NOAH (environmental movement) so militant and uncompromising.

Of course it is not a question of nuclear power in Denmark. Any enlightened human being can see that it is ridiculous to keep Denmark free of nuclear power stations because of the waste problem, when at the same time all other countries build nuclear power stations at a rapid pace. And no one at all believes seriously that »zero growth« will prevent us from running out of oil, it may at best postpone the oil exhaustion for a few years, while at the same time it will be disastrous to the developing countries, whom we also want to help. An element in the incoherent collection of opinions is, however, that the industrial countries have exploited the developing countries and therefore owe them a compensation, an assertion which is without an economic foundation. In the same way the assertion of resource exhaustion is without bearing reality and contrary to the opposition to nuclear power.

Briefly and to the point. The more radical and incoherent opinions, the greater chance of public success. For it is a question of something quite different, i.e. a new people's and »irrational« revolt against the elite, which is a safeguard of the experienced unreasonable and unjust social order. But God save the revolt from victory, which would result in the death of the movement, because of its obvious powerlessness towards the »actual conditions of iron industry« demanding the expert knowledge, which some people seem to despise.

However, being a continuous revolutionary movement it can keep the pot boiling for some time, and it may cause that the projects: EEC, nuclear power, natural gas, and so on will be considered once more, before the final decisions are made. And it is true that such decisions are irrevocable; a new technology and organization result in social changes, which make a reversible process impossible. For example the car cannot be abolished now without incalculable social consequences.

Like the salt to and the leaven in the bread those »grass root movements« will at one time be able to engage the public formation of opinions on what is good and bad and through their exaggerated criticism be able to activate politicians and technicians, i.e. the elite to use the utmost thoughtfulness before making radical social changes. It is true that there is without doubt a group of politically radical persons trying to fish in troubled waters, but the experiences from the universities show that they constitute a very small minority, and that they do not in the long run make up a real threat to democracy and to objectively defensible decisions.

But it may now and then be difficult to grasp the meaning of it all.

14

Notes

1) In the Scandinavian languages the word »meaning« also means intention, object, purpose.

2) See to the following *Stig Jørgensen*, Lovmål og Dom (1975), p. 9 ff., 74 ff.; *Justus Hartnack*, Den ny Filosofi, Berlingske leksikon Bibliotek (1963), p. 69. See also *A. Aarnio's* book, On Legal Reasoning, which in essential points harmonizes with my views.

3) See to the following, *Stig Jørgensen*, Samfundets syn på godt og ondt, Dansk Udsyn 1978, p. 313.

4) *Justus Hartnack*, l.c. (note 1) p. 71.

5) See *Nils Jareborg*, Värderingar (1975) and my review in Tidsskrift for Retsvæsen 1975, p. 613.

6) See *J. Dalberg-Larsen*, Retsvidenskaben som samfundsvidenskab (1977) Chap. 2.

7) See *Stig Jørgensen*, Modstandsret og ungdomsoprøret, Tidsskrift for Retsvæsen, årg. 1970 p. 198.

8) See *Stig Jørgensen*, Values in Law (1978), p. 148 ff.

9) *P. E. Mouritzen* and others, Borgerdeltagelse og græsrodsbevægelser. (Politica 1978).

10) *Stig Jørgensen*, Ret og samfundsdebat (1972), p. 107, see also Ugeskrift for Retsvæsen 1978 B, 141 ff.

11) See note 6 above.

Does Reality Exist?[1]

I rather think that someone might believe that I am completely out of my mind, or that I am trying to make fun of you. For it seems to be a question without any sense. Of couse reality exists; or how should I be able to write this?

The Danish author Svend Åge Madsen published a book some years ago with the title: »Sæt verden er til« (= Suppose the World Exists) (1971). It is about a man, who is reading a book about the books that he and his characters are writing. Each of them writes a book of his own and in doing so creates a world according to his own needs and ideas.

In these books certain persons and events recur; therefore it apparently cannot be a dream or fiction, as it is, I suppose, impossible to dream other person's dreams. Thus, reality seems to be after all, as something existing outside the books, and with which the books therefore deal. - Until you suddenly remember that there is only one writer writing about these books, and therefore he knows from the very start or rather has invented the reality described in the different books. So we do not receive any definite answer to the question, whether the world exists, or whether it is created by ourselves, as it is created by the author in his books.

Thus, the author's intention with his book is to draw attention to the fact that presumably there is something in the surrounding world and in our consciousness that we can see, hear and feel, and by means of our senses we are able to perceive and react to an outside world, such as is the case with animals and babies.

However, in order to be able to understand what we perceive these sense impressions have to be translated into a language that so to speak describes reality in a code which can be understood by the computer of the human brain. By means of the computer these impressions are worked up in what we call thoughts.[2]

The language[3] is the remarkable signalling system which no other species of animal but the human being has developed; and only the human being is able to transfer experiences and thoughts about these experiences from one individual to the other and from one generation to the other and thus create culture. Other

16

species of animal have signalling systems, by means of which they can communicate, call, threaten, warn, and so on, but they have no language, and consequently no consciousness. Recent experiments seem to indicate that the primates - the anthropoid apes - have certain very primitive faculties of thinking; they can take in more abstract information than signals, and therefore »understand« and solve - through thinking - more complex problems, for instance by means of tools.

However, the human cerebrum is abnormally enlarged compared with that of other animals, and a special ability to speak situated just behind the left temple has been developed. When this speech centre is hurt, either by a brain injury, a tumour or a haemorrhage, the human being can no longer speak, but the ability to think does not necessarily cease, because the ability to speak is lost, which the relatives of a brain-injured person should always bear in mind.

However, it is reasonable already now to point out the fact that the faculties of speech and reasoning are essentially attached to the left cerebral hemisphere, whereas the feelings, the sense, and the creative faculties are attached to the right cerebral hemisphere. This does not mean that the right hemisphere cannot think at all and the left hemisphere cannot feel at all; the fact is that a lot of connecting »threads« transfer information from the right to the left hemisphere and vice versa. However, the right cerebral hemisphere cannot speak!

A violent debate took place in Denmark in the middle of the 1970s, when a psychiatrist wrote that women's left cerebral hemisphere is less well-developed than that of men, and that women therefore think less logically and coherently. On the other hand, their right hemisphere was found to be better developed than that of men, which should explain the old prejudice that women have a better intuition; and thus without men's theoretical reasoning they can arrive at rational conclusions with somnambulistic certainty. I shall pay no more attention to this theory, which naturally is not very popular in these years of equality between the sexes.

The French author Joseph Ernest Renan has, however, affirmed this division of labour between the right and the left cerebral hemisphere. He describes his poetical creative procedure as a crowd of ideas and thoughts, which are screened by rational consideration.

By certain cerebral-physiological experiments in connection with the treatment of epileptics it has been demonstrated that an improvement arises when the connecting »threads« between the right and the left cerebral hemisphere are cut. Besides, by these experiments it was possible to obtain an insight in the function of such a »split brain«. - A visual impression was led through the left eye, which is connected with the right cerebral hemisphere. After that the person of the experiment was asked, what he saw; however, as the right cerebral hemisphere cannot speak, and the left one does not know what the right one has seen, the person talks nonsense, while the right hemisphere makes the person shake his head. If, then, a visual impression was led through the right eye to the left cerebral hemisphere, the person was able to answer, but his answer was often quite hasty and rash.

It is now possible to conceive reality in two completely different ways. We may look upon our senses as a camera and our consciousness as a film strip, currently reflecting objects in reality. However, we may also invert this model and consider our consciousness as a film projector, projecting our impressions on a large screen, which we then may call reality.

In the former way of considering reality we could regard our cognition as »objective«, i.e. valid to all human beings, who would therefore so to speak see the same pictures and call them the same names. This was the ideal of the theory of cognition named »logical empiricism« or »positivism«, because it conceived reality as something preexisting, which could be depicted and described unambiguously truly or falsely. And this was the very purpose of the theory, which intended to separate science from politics and religion.

And here we touch the very crux of the matter. If we do not look upon reality as something preexisting, but as something created by the individuals »projecting« their impressions out into the surrounding world, there will be no difference between dream and reality, and between fiction and reality.

The German idealism in the first half of the last century thought in fact that cognition had this »creative« character. In the romantic poetry, which was a further development of this idealism, it is the poet, who creates reality by virtue of his genius. The Danish romantic poet Adam Öehlenschläger's Alladin is the cheerful son of nature, who makes reality conform to his wishes by means of his magic lamp.

The subjectivity becomes the truth, as it was later said by the Danish philosopher Søren Kierkegaard. Thus, the truth is not objective - as assumed by positivism in its theory of reflection - in as much as it (i.e. the truth) depends on the person, who looks at it.

This dissension was a contributory cause to the youth revolt at the end of the 1960s. In the post-war era there had been a tendency to accept life as it was, because it was important to re-establish the societies after the destructions of the war. Thus, there was an inclination to consider economic growth as the crucial and almost »objective« value in life, so that the object of politics and human activity as a whole had to be to increase the prosperity in society. Consequently, there was a tendency to conceive our acts as more or less »appropriate« without further precision.

18

Then a so-called »critical« science called in question the assumption that material values and economic growth alone were self-evident truths. The German-American sociologist Herbert Marcuse spoke of »the one-dimensional human being« and emphasized that »the whole human being« consists of feeling as well as intelligence. Freedom, he said, is more important than material goods; therefore, the essential thing is to organize the society in such a way that oppression is eradicated. As the Capitalist system in his opinion was an oppressing system, because it subordinated human beings to the material production, he argued in favour of a new Marxism, which by the abolition of private property of the means of production would free human beings from the oppression of production, as it was possible now to adapt production to the simple needs of human beings.

It is quite understandable that such a theory had an enormous influence on a generation of young people, who had never been in want, and who had never known the horrors of war and the Nazist and Communist tyrannies with their total control of the human consciousness.

They represented a generation of young people, who had received a good education on the one hand, but was taught, in accordance with the theory of motivation, to make demands on the methods of the school on the other. It was not the pupils' fault, if they had not learnt enough; the teachers were to blame, because they had not been capable of motivating the pupils sufficiently. The main thing was no longer to achieve what you may call »concrete knowledge«, but to be able to »understand« the coherence in things. Consequently, the separation of the subject matters was abolished; subjects like history, geography, biology and so on were replaced by »social studies«, «natural studies«, and »general studies«; »project work« and »group work« were meant to »activate« the pupils and to make them understand the importance of »co-operation«. In the subject »Danish« it was found to be more important to stimulate an oral delivery than to develop a correct spelling and punctuation.

By giving a higher priority to understanding and motivation than to knowledge and the performance of the individual, this kind of schooling will naturally displace the pupils' self-knowledge and make them place the responsibility on the »system«, i.e. the school system, the social system. A »critical« attitude, which is a consequence of the tendency to make a maximum of demands on others and a minimum on oneself, will easily develop into a general dissatisfaction, if it goes together with a decreasing actual understanding of reality and the functioning of natural and social laws.

And this was just the case, as in the first place the technical as well as the social development had created completely new and complicated mechanisms, which were difficult to deal with; secondly the school system did no longer qualify the pupils to understand these coherences.

Thus, the protest against a materialistic attitude and authoritarian and oppressing institutions - which were imputed to the older generation by the young people - assumed the form of a »criticism« of a »positivist« theory of science. This theory was said to be conservative and »reactionary«, because it did not go beyond »describing« the positively given reality. The older generation only asked: how? and not: why?, or rather: why not?, i.e. why are things - especially social conditions - as they are, and why aren't they organized in another way?

Therefore, science and consequently our whole cognition were claimed to be »political«. »Positivism«, i.e. the theory of reflection, is reactionary, whereas »critical science«, i.e. the theory of projection, is revolutionary and liberating. Thus, it lay near at hand for those young people to consider all acts with the purpose of changing society as »scientific«.

»Action research« was a new idea, which consisted in making the population conscious, i.e. change its consciousness, so that it »realized« that the right thing to do was to change society in a »liberating« direction. According to »New Marxism« it could be proved scientifically that Socialism would necessarily occur when the oppressing character of private property was abolished, and that the consciousness reflects the material system of production in society. Nevertheless the supporters of this theory found that they had to further this development by influencing the consciousness of the population in this direction by means of different actions.

Of great importance was the new mass medium, which during the 1960s had made its entry into most homes. TV brought pictures of »reality« directly into people's homes, and so to speak turned reality into pictures, into films. It is a question whether it was the youth revolt that deliberately exploited the ability and limitation of the TV-medium to transform reality into pictures, or whether it was the very conditions of the TV-medium that led to an extremely close coverage of these »actions«.

At any rate it is quite obvious that it was the fortunate meeting of incidence and possibility that conditioned the success of the youth revolt as well as of TV. Very quickly it was learnt how to arrange a »happening« or a »pseudo-event«, i.e. something that did not really take place, but has been arranged for the sake of TV. Just as the consciousness according to the theory of projection cannot distinguish between fiction and reality, the TV-medium cannot distinguish between real events and »pseudo-events«. The arranged reality has just as much reality as has the »real« one. »Active report« and »engaged journalism« have become the ideals of a new generation of journalists.

However, the reasoning goes further than that. »News« is in principle something that takes place where journalists are present, i.e. journalists who are in a position to write and publish what they see. In the areas of the world, which are not covered by journalists, there will consequently be no »news«, just as America did not exist for the Europeans, until it was »discovered« by Columbus.

In practice this means that nothing happens in the politically uninteresting parts of the world, whereas a lot of things happens, where the journalists are present beforehand owing to considerable political problems. For instance the Vietnam War and the crises in the Middle East (respectively) was and is covered very closely by the world press; this is the reason why many more things take place here, which do not take place elsewhere, because the press is not present beforehand.

In two of his latest novels the German author Heinrich Böll has dealt with the cruel inclination of the press to create human tragedies in a good cause. This may happen, when the private life of chance persons becomes a public matter, because the press and the police as a precaution supervise or protect certain persons or groups. In his latest book: »Fürsorgliche Belagerung«, a woman neighbour of a family being protected by the police gets her affair with another man than her husband disclosed, when the police investigates her friend's »suspicious« conduct. The result is that the lives of three persons are ruined. - In the other book: »Die verlorene Ehre der Katharina Blum«, it is also a stray acquaintance with a wanted terrorist that arouses the unwanted interest of the press and the police.

Here we touch on an essential point: our cognition of »reality« depends on the fact that somebody is present, who can show or tell what is going on. This will necessarily result in a distortion of the proportions, owing to our »interest« in knowing something. If there are no journalists present we shall not be informed, but if there for some reason happens to be journalists in the vicinity, we shall hear quite a lot which does not have anything to do with the reason why they are present.

However, there is also another side of the matter. If the press has no access or is not allowed to say what it wants, we shall not be informed either, even if we might be interested, and in case we hear anything, the information will be faked.

For instance we received a steady flow of words and picture from the Vietnam War, in fact we heard and saw so much that it is seriously claimed that TV is to thank or blame for the defeat of the USA in Vietnam, as a democracy cannot fight wars before open TV-cameras. However, we do not receive any information from the war in Afghanistan, and if we do, it will be heavily censored words and pictures reflecting the rulers' interest in concealing »reality«, if it does not suit them.

The press has therefore been called the fourth power of state besides the legislative, the executive, and the judicial power, because it - by spreading information and opinions - enables the authorities to perform their tasks. This is the reason why freedom of the press in a democracy is extremely important, whereas it is inadmissible in a dictatorship. Freedom of the press and democracy are the counterparts of the »theory of reflection«, inasmuch as the press ideally takes care of the collection and publishing of information about »reality«, so that the population is able to size up »reality« and in so doing influence their politicians. Censorship of the press and dictatorship are on the other hand the counterparts of the »theory of projection«, inasmuch as it is the rulers' picture of »reality«, which is projected out into society. In a democracy the people elects new leaders, if they lose the people's confidence, whereas in a dictatorship - Bertold Brecht said - the leaders if so elect a new people. By this he ironically meant that the population's consciousness is (deliberately) changed by means of the press and the police.

Thus, it is true that our cognition is dependent on interests, inasmuch as in a democracy we only hear about the things, which somebody takes an interest in investigating and telling about, and inasmuch as in a dictatorship we hear only about the things, which the rulers take an interest in telling about. However, it is true that also in a democracy the media may be abused by journalists, who for political or personal reasons are interested in telling or concealing a story or in representing it in a distorted way. Finally, it is also possible - by exploiting the knowledge of the conditions of the press and TV - to make a piece of »news«, whose only purpose is to force the press to devote its time to a certain case. The hunger strikes in prisons in Northern Ireland were a cruel example of this strategy; another way to attract the attention of the press is to seize hostages, a method which is used very often nowadays and all over the world.

However, for a moment we have to return to the linguistic treatment of reality, for even the TV-medium is dependent on texts and commentaries; if it had not been for the texts and commentaries the camera lens and its perspectives would alone be decisive of the »reality« that we see on TV. However, there is an important fundamental difference between the linguistic description and the pure pictorial influence of our consciousness: the linguistic description is worked up in the left cerebral hemisphere, whereas the pictures directly influence the right passive cerebral hemisphere.

In the USA some investigations have been made of the function and influence of the TV-medium on the American social life. These investigations seem to prove that the TV-medium is well suited for advertising and for political and similar influence. A message can easily be brought into our consciousness: by sending a series of pictures into the right - uncritical - cerebral hemisphere and at the same time cut off the intellectual and linguistic working up - either by sending the pictures in very short moments or by diverting people's attention by irrelevant talk.

In fact, it has been demonstrated that quite a number of children - especially from the most unfavourable environments - is sent to school almost without a language, as they have spent most of their childhood watching TV; pictures have been sent directly into their non-linguistic right hemisphere, while the linguistic left hemisphere has literally been on a holiday. Before the TV-medium was introduced children had to take care of their own entertainment either through activity and play or through reading. - In both cases they would have to use the language, which demands an active and critical thinking. Unfortunately, this situation has in the post-war era been replaced by a passive, nonlinguistic and thus unthinking entertainment, which leaves the children as robots without a language.

And here we face the greatest danger to education in the future and thus to democracy, which demands a high educational level.[4] Thus, the fact is that the TV-medium in itself - i.e. whatever the intention - creates an inclination to passivity and especially to a weakening of the development of the faculty of speech. Consequently, the language becomes poor, inaccurate and crude; for instance the language of the media seems to lack the sense of proportions.

It is a bad thing not being able to express one's thoughts quite clearly, because - as the Swedish poet Esaias Tegnér said more than 100 years ago - obscure speaking is due to obscure thinking. Or, in other words, if you have lost the ability to speak or express yourself precisely, you will not be able to think clearly. And if you cannot think clearly, you cannot act rationally.

A population only being accustomed to watching pictures instead of using its language and intelligence will be more than usually inclined to turn its criticism into general discontent or violence. The fact is that violence starts where the talking ends, and the treshold of tolerance will grow still lower, in case we passively allow TV and the so-called »audio-visual« aids and similar modern pedagogics to replace the linguistic analysis and criticism. You may go so far as to say that only what you yourself have set down in writing is correctly understood.

For reality must - as already mentioned - be described, whether we believe in it or not. Even though it exists already - as we seem to think, when we hit our heads against a wall - it has to be translated into words and concepts, before it can be understood by the computer of the human brain. It (i.e. reality) cannot be received, until it has been translated into the language, to which the brain is coded.

If this is not the case, it will go directly into the right cerebral hemisphere, where it is stowed away without further working up. If the thinking, i.e. the computer system of our consciousness, shall be able to work up, screen, and criticize our sense data, these have to be described, and preferably as precisely as possible; otherwise the action programme will not have the desired effect, i.e. lead to the desired ends with the smallest possible number of mistakes.

Indeed, the language is not just an objective tool translating sense data into electric impulses like TV-signals. It follows from what has been written above that the language is active; when you »describe« reality, you also create it to a certain degree. Just as God named the things and in doing so said something about their »nature«, we also put something of ourselves into the things, when we name them. For instance the very same person may be called a »patriot« by some people and a »terrorist« by other people. The hunger strikes in Northern Ireland is for instance in a sense a dispute about mere words, as the imprisoned members of the IRA want to be considered as political prisoners, whereas the British authorities treat them like ordinary criminals.

Our political, religious, cultural, and esthetic evaluations will necessarily be reflected in the concepts that we use about the things, and this is also true of our general needs and interests. A »table« is for instance an appliance to put things on, while a »chair« is an appliance to sit on. Those, who have read Jonathan Swift's book »Gulliver's travels«, will remember the comic situation, when having tied Gulliver the Lilliputs begin to search his pockets and for instance describe a tobacco jar and a pistol, although they do not know the concepts: snuffing and shooting.

In fact there are no »pipes« and »matches« in »reality«, the same is true of »horses« and »cows«, »woods«, »trees«, »tables« or »chairs«. However, there are some objects, animals, and constructions that we »call« these names, by means of which we are able to think over and talk about such things. They are translated into »general concepts«, which are abstractions from reality, like the figures between 0 and 10, and which therefore can be received by the computer of the brain, which is coded with those »concepts« in the same way as the calculating machine is coded with figures.

The concepts, of which the language consists, are thus the elements, of which the thinking consists. The left cerebral hemisphere is, as mentioned, meant to make the intellectual and linguistic working up of reality, while the right one popularly perceives picture and screens the proposals for understanding and action, which are the results of the process of thought.

Thus, our whole process of cognition is »linguistic«, in the sense that we cannot consider anything that is not translated into language. Therefore, we must conclude that »reality« exists and does not exist. There is an infinity of things and powers in the universe, and it would be foolish to confuse fantasy with reality. This was exactly what the Danish author Hans Egede Schack described in the first modern Danish novel: »Phantasterne« (= The Fantasts) (1857).

However, it is true that we create our life partly by naming it and by considering it. - As language is the condition of human culture, it is consequently very important that we develop and preserve the language that we have got as a precious tool, which should be »sharpened« instead of being »blunted«. We must realize that our language is not »objective«, but is coloured by our interests and our needs. On the other hand, our language will lose its value as a means of communication, if we do not endeavour as far as possible to use the words in the same meaning. In case of disagreement about the realities we should not conceal it - either consciously or unconsciously - by means of vague and unprecise language; instead we should make clear the disagreement by analysing the different meanings of the words.

If we do not insist on the precision in our language, we shall become either executioners or victims in the struggle for souls, taking place on the political, religious and cultural market of opinions. And in case the linguistic consciousness is replaced by a world of pictures, like the one on TV, there is a danger that people will lose their language some time in the future. If this happened they would be defenceless against all those, who for commercial, political or religious reasons intend to make »reality« look in a certain way. This reality would go directly into their right cerebral hemisphere, without leaving them any chance of self-defence.

What young people of today should be told is: Beware of the language. Beware of the »reality«, which is presented to you by the written and especially by the electronic media. In any case this »reality« consists of more or less haphazard »segments« of reality, which are a result of a series of random choices and choices based on interests. The reality being presented is therefore »fragmentary«, i.e. incoherent and without proportions. Particularly the TV-medium is inclined to choose photogenic, dramatic and personal events, so that the abstract coherence, the undramatic normal state and the general social perspective are superseded.

This being so the already existing difficulty in understanding the complicated reality will be intensified and give rise to »frustration«, i.e. powerlessness, aggression, and violence or passivity. Nowadays we see many examples of frustration, for instance criminality, terrorism, protest-movements, protest-parties and various kinds of action on the one hand, and drug addiction, hippy movements and a romanticizing of the rural life and so on on the other.

I suppose, many of these features, which form a part of the development since the 1960s, are positive, but many are absolutely negative. And they are not connected only with the development in the mass media and our description of reality, but neither are they unaffected by these things. We cannot reverse the development and return to the secure reality of the past. However, we may try - by cultivating our language and critical sense - to reduce the damaging consequences of the electronic media and the popular press, when they appeal to our lowest instincts.

In fact the human being is not as bad as people think, and not at all as bad as its reputation.

Notes

1) Karl Larenz' philosophical strive in his philosophy of science has always been the attempt to bridge »positivism« and »phenomenology«. He has stressed the predominant importance of valuations within legal science and legal practice (Methodenlehre der Rechtswissenschaft, 4. Aufl. 1979, p. 193). He has emphasized that description of the circumstances of the concrete case as well as interpretation of the legal rules depend on valuations, and that the judicial decision is therefore the result of a decision and not of a logical deduction (loc.cit. Chap. 3 and 4-5). He refers primarily to the »open« character of the »type concept« (loc.cit. Chap. 6), but stresses that the valuations must not go beyond the framework of the »positive legal system«; on the other hand, however, the legal principles are a part of »positive law«, as they are the result of the cultural development within a given political reality (loc.cit. Chap. 6, and Richtiges Recht, 1979, p. 174 ff.).
On all these essential points I agree with Karl Larenz (see Recht und Gesellschaft, 1970; Vertrag und Recht, 1968, p. 90 ff., p. 111 ff.; Typologie und Realismus, in: Nachrichten der Akademie der Wissenschaften in Göttingen, 1971; Norm und Wirklichkeit, in: Rechtstheorie, 1971, p. 1 ff.; Values in Law, 1978, p. 9 ff., p. 29 ff., p. 135 ff., and p. 151 ff. (p. 168)).
This article - dealing with the fundamental problems of cognition and description of »reality« - therefore belongs naturally in a festschrift in honour of Karl Larenz.
2) See Stig Jørgensen, Norm und Wirklichkeit (loc.cit. note 1), in: Rechtstheorie, 1971, p. 1-16; Ideology and Science, in: Scandinavian Studies in Law, 18, 1974, p. 87-107; (Values in Law, 1978, p. 9 ff., and p. 151-176); On Meaning, Opinion and Argumentation, in: Peczenik, A. - Uusitalo (Eds.), Reasoning on Legal Reasoning, 1979, p.87-94; Hermeneutik und Auslegung, in: Rechtstheorie, 1978, p. 63-72; Law and Society, 1972, Chap. 1 and 4.
3) See to the following, Det lærde Selskabs Publikationsserie, Ny Serie (Ed.: Stig Jørgensen) No. 2: Sprog og virkelighed (= Language and Reality), 1972; No. 3: Ideologi og videnskab (= Ideology and Science), 1973; and No. 7-8: Symmetri i videnskaberne (= Symmetry in the Sciences), 1975.
4) See Stig Jørgensen, Demokratiets dilemma (= The Dilemma of Democracy) (12 papers), 1981.

Basic Norm and Paradox

I. Introduction

The purpose of this article is to ease the discussion of »the basic norm« having Hans Kelsen's legal philosophy as a starting point, and to show that jurists in other spheres have solved problems of the same kind without much difficulty. I shall try to prove that the problem of the basic norm - which Kelsen originally realized - is a logical problem (the theory of condition), but by changing his theory (the theory of fiction) later on Kelsen showed that he had attached a greater importance to the basic norm than one might have expected.

Kelsen's merits were that in continuation of Kant and the logical positivistic theory of science he clarified the epistemological separation of the world of reality, which is ruled by the law of causation and the consequent necessity, and the world of norms, which is ruled by the principle of liberty and the consequent responsibility. He maintained therefore that it is impossible to come from »is« to »ought« and that the norms, including the legal norms as well, cannot be derived from reality but must be »imputated under« a higher norm. In order to avoid an infinite regress Kelsen introduced a »basic norm« being superior to the constitution and the legal system.[1]

My point is that Kelsen's logical condition has a function which goes beyond the logical - or tautological - one, on which any logical system is based. It has like the grounds legitimating natural law in superior material principles of value also a legitimating function which as mentioned above appears especially in Kelsen's later change of the status of the basic norm into a »fiction«.[2]

It is my opinion that the later debate has been fixed on this extra-systematic function of legitimation and thus has been concentrated on the status of these external factors, the logical aspect being relegated to the background. In this respect it is interesting that Herbert Hart who originally formulated a general theory about the open character of ideas and concepts and especially legal concepts: their »defeasibility« which contained the key to the understanding of the logical status of »the basic norm« as a tautological condition, later on rejected this conception and adopted Kelsen's theory of basic norm, giving the basic norm (rule of recognition) an empiric status, which was no improvement in my opinion.[3]

As mentioned, jurists are familiar with tautological grounds since for instance it does not normally disturb them both making the concept of »unlawful« a condition of a sanction and conditioning it by the sanction. Alf Ross has actually wanted to regard the idea of rights as a »tool of representation« which connects a »legal fact« with a »legal consequence«.[4]

In the following I shall try to explain in detail the logical coherence between the idea of the basic norm, the paradox problem, and the general conceptual analysis. From a common-sense assumption that contradictions in the thinking are due to semantic circumstances, or to be more explicit, inaccuracies or uncertainties in the linguistic wording, I shall begin with some clear examples of such semantic errors and I shall then indicate that the errors have a more fundamental background in the open character of the language and that the solution of the problems therefore must be found along these lines.

II. Logic, Semantics and Paradox

The Dano-Norwegian Professor Ludvig Holberg (1684-1754) whose first work published was a textbook of natural law in the manners of the time[5] satirized in a number of literary juvenile works the religious, political, and cultural orthodoxy of that time. In one of his comedies, Erasmus Montanus, Holberg takes it out on the scholastic method of science which ruled the universities right up to the 18th century.[6]

During a stay in his home village Erasmus Montanus, a young and ridiculous student, impresses and terrorizes his family and his friends with his false syllogisms. One of the tragi-comic culminations of the play occurs when he in the following way proves that his mother is a stone:

> A stone cannot fly
> *mother Karen cannot fly*
> ergo mother Karen is a stone,

a proof which naturally leads to both sorrow and anger. It does not get better when he proves that the parish clerk is a cock:

> A cock can crow
> *the parish clerk can crow*
> ergo the parish clerk is a cock

since it makes the village get angry with him when the stupid parish clerk gets the sympathy of the villagers by defending the obvious truth that the earth is flat as a pancake and not - as claimed by Erasmus - round like a ball.

With this loose introduction to the analysis of an important legal theoretical problem I wish to draw attention to the risks of logic. Of course no scientist would commit the above-mentioned fatal errors when applying the laws of logic. But nevertheless it is not quite superfluous to draw attention to the semantic problems of logic.

Paradoxes[7] may be apparent contradictions, i.e. a logical structure, which seems to force us to assume opposite things.

The classic wording is the Crete Epimenides' paradox: »All Cretes lie«. He either speaks the truth and then he is lying, or he lies and then he is speaking the truth! Paradoxes can be reduced to the well-known wording:

»This sentence is false«!

or with a bitter-sweet twist in the stately declaration on the title page of a bibliographical work:

»This book contains no mispirnts«!

However, the latter sentence points out the dissolution of the paradox indicating the semantic ambiguity which is in other cases hidden in the apparently very clear words and ideas.

In other cases it is just as clear according to the coherence that the paradoxical wording is due to the fact that keywords are used in different meanings. When for instance it says in the Danish translation of the New Testament (Matthew, Chap. 16, v. 25):

»For the one who will save his life shall lose it; but the one who loses his life shall save it.«

There is no doubt that »life« means »physical life« and »eternal life«, respectively. It is actually explained (Matthew, Chap. 13, v. 11-13) that parables are necessary to explain the deepest meaning of the teaching to those who are not already seeing.

It is also clear that Holberg's above-mentioned syllogisms are false because they offend against the rules of logical conclusions partly by inferring from negative premises partly by changing subject and predicate. From the sentence: »You castigate the one you love« we cannot infer that we love all the ones we hit.

Ever since Aristotle it has been known that certain logical conclusions can be drawn only from universals which are defined unambiguously and that you cannot deduce more from these than you have already read into them. Consequently you can with certainty move down (deductively) or up (inductively) in a logical system. On the other hand you cannot in that way give the grounds for the first fundamental premiss which is provided by another method than the rational one; it is set (arbitrarily) by means of the ability which Aristotle calls *nous*, and Kant later on called *intuition*.

Naturally, a logical system cannot be based on logic, i.e. by means of arguments which are taken within the framework of the system. It would be an error of category (a confusion of different logical categories) if it was tried to do so. On the other hand it would also be an error of category to base or justify a logical system on arguments outside this system. Any logical system is autonomous so to speak, and cannot have, nor does it need any internal or external grounds or »legitimation«.

On the other hand it is also clear that a logical system only allows certain conclusions because it is a linguistic conceptual system. This was the reason why Descartes limited science to the world of thought. Certainty is however obtained at the expense of the attachment to reality since in the world of reality nothing happens with certainty but only with probability. Even Aristotle was aware of the dualism between language and reality (analytika priori and posteriori) meaning, however, that it was possible to establish a connection since ideas in his opinion were characteristics of the things in reality. It was therefore important to find out »the nature« of things, i.e. the ideal state for which the things were striving.

III. Theory of Science

However, Hume and Kant disposed of this metaphysics definitively and maintained categorically that laws of nature cannot be proved but only made probable and that the values are not characteristics of the things either. Thus it is not possible to come from an »is« to an »ought«. As we know Kant's solution of this dilemma was to *presume* that, i.a. the law of causation was a necessary condition of cognition for the external world and that the free will was a necessary condition of responsibility for the internal world.

In our century logical empiricism has revived this theory of cognition and made the experience a criterion of truth. If something that corresponds to the linguistic expression is found in the world of experience it is true; otherwise it is false. It is clear that you cannot compare a linguistic conception with an unlinguistic reality just like that. Thus the reality which is to verify a linguistic expression must first be *qualified* in the same system of language. The are no insuperable difficulties in such a refined *theory of correspondance*. According to its own rules the same system of language, which is the criterion of truth according to a *theory of coherence*, can be used for a description of the reality which can then be compared with the statement to be verified.

The price of treating reality scientifically or in other words: attaching science to reality - which must probably be the purpose of science if it is to be of any use - is our acceptance of the varying degrees of subjectivity that a description of reality governed by human purposes and interests necessarily implies.[8] The fact that man's thoughts practically correspond to reality is in principle arbitrary, but probably not accidental, man (and thus his thought) being a part of the reality that is structuralized by the thought.

Logical empiricism also accepted Kant's other axiom: that »ought« cannot be inferred from »is«. The »tied« world of facts and legalities belongs to another category than the »free« world of actions and responsibility. It is beyond the purpose of this paper to show that this, in principle, right assumption need not have disastrous consequences for the rationality of judicial decisions and decisions in general. There is nothing to prevent us from assuming that the rational process - leading to the final syllogism, in which the decision can be described as a logical inference from the rule of law: If p then q (p > q) and description of legal facts: »p« to the legal consequence »q« - is corresponded by an empiric psychological process of thought, of which i.a. an experience of duty and validity corresponding the linguistic description forms part.[9]

IV. Dissolution of the Paradox

If we return to the starting point, the logical paradox, it is now possible to see that the apparent contradiction may be due to other semantic problems than the very simple ones, which we have been considering. We must not forget that logic only says something true about reality if the premisses are true in relation to reality, and if there is a complete or perhaps a certain limited identity in the subject of the sentences. The question here is, i.a. whether the paradox of the liar is due only to an imprecise description.

At any rate that is the way in which it is tried to dissolve the paradox. When a Crete says that all Cretes lie it is possible to understand the situation in such a way that the person speaking acts on the general phrase: all those present excepted. In other words: The one who speaks is not speaking about himself even though the sentence might give us that impression. When he says: »all«, he means in other words, »all« except me, at least in this sentence.[10] In the same way J. C. Hicks (note 7, p. 278) dissolves the paradox about Achilles and the tortoise. He (Achilles) will *never* catch up with the hundred meters' start of the tortoise even if he runs ten times as fast because the tortoise will always be ahead according to the series $100+10+1+0,1+0,01$ ..... which *never* ends. In the first case »never« means something *temporal* but not in the other case; here it refers to the *number* of links in the series and not to the *sum* or the distance.

Another objection against the liar paradox is often used, namely that a sentence cannot be about itself. Alf Ross maintained that on these grounds section 88 of the Danish Constitution dealing with the procedure of constitutional amendments cannot be a part of the constitution.[11] Others have seen the same problem in the English theory of the sources of law: Partly the rule that Parliament can pass anything, partly the rule that the courts of law are bound by their previous decisions.

Say can Parliament restrict its own competence by deciding that a given Statute is to be unchangeable? Say could the House of Lords by means of its Practice Statement of July 26th 1966 decide that it would no longer be bound by its previous decision?

In all three examples the linguistic expressions contain the same logical structure which is apparently either self-contradictory or self-referring. Therefore the solution must in all cases be found in the same analysis which dissolves the logical dilemma or shows that the sentences, being about themselves, are not completely empty.

In the discussion about section 88 of the Danish Constitution the late professor of philosophy and logic at the University of Aarhus, Niels Egmont Christensen, stated as opposed to Alf Ross that section 88 is not *only* self-referring, but refers to the whole Danish Constitution and is therefore *also* about itself, but only to an insignificant extent and accidentally so to speak. The rule of amendment, he says, is therefore far from empty and from a common-sense point of view there is therefore no reason to draw the absurd conclusion that the rule of amendment is not a part of the Danish Constitution.[12] By using Russell's argument it would also be possible to get out of the dilemma by drawing attention to the semantic difference between the type of rules which are rules in the proper sense of the word, and the type of rules which are rules of competence. Therefore an omnipotent Parliament cannot decide that its statutes are to be unchangeable, and therefore on the other hand, a court creating precedents cannot decide that its decisions in the future are not to be binding for itself.

Indeed there must be a supposition that logical inferences being in defiance of common sense are the result of a semantic error in the apparently identical linguistic expressions. Until his death the above-mentioned Niels Egmont Christensen worked at an interesting project, namely to prove that even the totally formal mathematical logic was illogical because of a till then overlooked difference in the sense of the sign of »or« (v) which could be either »strong«, i.e. containing an exclusive alternative (»it is either raining or not«) or »weak«, i.e. not containing a clear alternative (»it is either raining or New York is a big city«). Only in the former case is it possible to draw true logical conclusions whereas in the latter there is a possibility of falling into fallacies.[13]

Unfortunately the writer's theory was not discussed internationally before he died so that he might have arrived at a certain knowledge of whether his theory about these fundamental semantic weaknesses of the formal logic was valid. But at the first glance it seems plausible to a non-expert that there may be such an explanation of certain dilemmas in logic though this analysis cannot explain all of them. Niels Egmont Christensen also drew attention to the fact that the difficulties of the general logic of truth did not always touch the normative logic which is not attached to reality in the same way.[14]

V. Tautology and »Defeasibility«

In other branches of law we are familiar with the logical problems which make »the problem of the basic norm« look so awe-inspiring, especially because great personalities like Hans Kelsen, H. L. A. Hart, and Alf Ross have been affected by this and fought their ways to solutions which seem forced, and besides, are different. On the other hand it is also with a certain hesitation that one presents one's own simple analysis which makes the problem a hackneyed problem that the jurists have been living with in so many other spheres. It is my opinion that one shall not look for the reasons for the validity of law in cases outside the legal system neither in a higher value like natural law (God, sense, intuition)[15], in the »basic norm« of Hans Kelsen whether it is called a »logical condition«[16] or a »fiction«[17], in a feeling of obligation or other psycho-social circumstances like the realistic theories of for instance Alf Ross[18] nor in a »rule of recognition« meaning a social fact like in Herbert Hart.[19]

Hans Kelsen and Herbert Hart agree that an »obligation« is a special logical category which differs from the feelings and the behaviour which correspond with the »duty« in the real world. A duty can therefore not be »derived« from a fact, but can, as Kelsen points out, only be derived from a norm which can only be derived from a higher norm.[20] In Kelsen's first interpretation of the basic norm of the pure theory of law, it is almost as a »logical condition« in Kant's way whereas his later reinterpretation into a »fiction« was not any step forward (in my opinion).[21] Towards Ross Hart normally maintains that »obligation« is a logical category separated from the binding consciousness, however, he ends up with identifying the »basic norm« (rule of recognition) as something social or political, i.e. custom, constitution and Parliament, revolution, etc.[22] Hart himself has described his theory as a kind of »descriptive sociology«, especially he wants to reject any validity based on natural law and to maintain a legal positivistic starting point in order to distinguish between law and morality.

The matter is, however, so simple that a system of duties can logically be based only on itself and that the grounds therefore *necessarily* must be tautological. On the other hand it is also a situation we know from other parts of the legal system.

In the teaching of the source of law it has been discussed whether the »metalegal« principles which underlie our legal system and governs out normative argumentation are a part of the legal system or not.[23] But in the dogmatic law as well the problem is well-known. For instance it is - as mentioned above - well-known in the law of torts and criminal law in Scandinavia that a sanction is attached to an anlawful action which is defined in relation to the sanction. In the law of contract it is normal to talk about promises as binding legal transactions and still talk about invalid or non-binding promises. With an expression borrowed from Herbert Hart it may be said that all legal conceptions are »defeasible«, i.e. must be understood with reservations which are a part of the legal system as well.[24]

The example show that the jurists are used to working with the paradoxical duality between validity and invalidity and between legal and extra legal norms meaning that certain conceptions in certain respects are conceived as a part of the system and in other respects are conceived as »metasystematic«. The contradiction is dissolved by the simple principle that logical systems must necessarily be tautological.

VI. Norm and Reality

When is a legal system, i.e. considered as system, fundamentally changed?, or, as formulated in the theory: When is the »basic norm« changed? is of course a practically important question. It is, as Kelsen emphasized, especially revolutions which all at once change the basis of the »validity« of the legal system by virtue of the change of the political system when the revolution has conquered, with the result that the population obeys the new government voluntarily or involuntarily. In recent times the development in Rhodesia has demonstrated that this problem as well has an internal and an external perspective.[25]

After the secession of Rhodesia from the British Empire the legislation of the new government was internally regarded as »valid« as the Rhodesian Supreme Court adopted the statutes though two judges of the Supreme Court resigned; whereas externally it was regarded as invalid by the British Empire.[26] By refusing to recognize the secession of Rhodesia in spite of the success of the revol-

34

ution England made use of a legal or quasilegal argumentation in a political struggle which, however, ended successfully at the final change to majority rule through English agency.

The question is of course of great political, social and cultural importance, but it is just as clear that from a legal and legal-theoretical point of view it is a question of limited importance. The question of the validity of the legal system is a question of the existence of the system. When, why, and how the system was established is in this respect without importance since the grounds of the system can only be found within the system itself.

Another question of great practical interest for the »validity« of the legal system is its »efficiency«. As we know, Kelsen claimed that together with the formal validity of the legal system another claim on the rules of law must be made, namely that they must be »effective«, sanctioned obligations.[27]

Especially Alf Ross has criticized this confusion of a »purely« normative conception of law with an idea of efficiency which is connected with (or is identical with) the conception of the State. Ross operates with a dualistic legal idea, operating on the one hand with a formal *idea of validity* which involves the existence of legal duties and on the other with a real *idea of being valid* which assumes that the rules of law are actually used. But Ross is in a way consistently a realist as he identifies »validity« with the normative ideology of the judges.[28]

But again we have to say that the question of the »efficiency« of its actual existence (»Geltung«) is a problem of another category than the »validity« of law. And the ideas and the experiences of obligation of the citizens and the authorities or their behaviour in accordance with these are also irrelevant compared to the »existence« of law. I shall not take a decision on the ontological question about the status of »existence« and about »validity« and »existence« which in Kelsen may be of the same status.[29] On the other hand, a condition of a positivistic conception of law is to be able to regard at the same time the rules of law as »existing« positive phenomena which can be made the subject of an external description and as a normative obligation which from within may be made the subject of a dogmatic-exegetic interpretation.[30]

Notes

1) General Theory of Law and State (1945) p. 117, 396, 437.
2) Allgemeine Theorie der Normen (1979) p. 216.
3) Cf. note 19, 21, and 23 below.
4) »Tu-Tu«, 70 Harvard Law Review (1956-57) p. 812 ff., On Law and Justice (1958) Ch. 6.
5) *Ludvig Holberg*, Introduktion til Natur- og Folkeretten (1716).

6) See *Stig Jørgensen*, Entwicklung und Methode des Privatrechts, Vertrag und Recht (1968) p. 57 f.

7) See *J. C. Hicks*, The Liar Paradox in Legal Reasoning, Cambridge Law Journal (1971) p. 275 ff.

8) *Stig Jørgensen*, Ideology and Science, Values in Law (1978) p. 9 ff.

9) *Stig Jørgensen*, Values in Law (1978) p. 151 ff., and *same*, Die rechtliche Entscheidung und ihre Begründung, Rhetorische Rechtstheorie (Festschrift für Theodor Viehweg) (1981) p. 337, see also *same*, Recht und Gesellschaft (1971) p. 13 ff. and 89 ff., *same*, Typologie und Realismus, Nachrichten der Akademie der Wissenschaften in Göttingen, I. Philologisch-historische Klasse (1971) Nr. 3, *same*, Norm und Wirklichkeit, Rechtstheorie (1971) 1 ff.

10) At any rate this is the solution Bertrand Russell looked for, Mathematical Logic as based on the Theory of Types, 30 American Journal of Mathematic 222 (here is quoted from: *J. C. Hicks*, The Liar Paradox in Legal Reasoning, l.c. (note 7) p. 275 ff.; see also *N. J. Jamieson*, Status to Contract, Cambridge Law Journal (1980) p. 357 f.

11) *Alf Ross*, »On Self-Reference and a Puzzle in Constitutional Law« (1969) p. 78, vol. 1, Dansk Statsforfatningsret I, 2nd ed. (1966) p. 176 ff., *Hicks*, l.c. (note 7) p. 280.

12) *Niels Egmont Christensen*, Er Grundlovens § 88 en del af grundloven, Juristen (1960) p. 231 ff.; see also *Torstein Eckhoff* and *Nils Kristian Sundby*, Om selvrefererende lover, Tidsskrift for Rettsvitenskap (1974) p. 34 ff.

13) *Niels Egmont Christensen*, Logik, ulogisk logik og ontologi, Philosophia 7 (1978) p. 33 ff.

14) Besides he agreed with *Ilmar Tammelo* and *Hans Kelsen* that in principle there is no difference between the logic of truth and normative logic that there is a need for some special deontic logic. - L.c. (note 12) p. 237. - *Ilmar Tammelo*, I. Tammelo/Helmut Schreiner, Grundzüge und Grundverfahren der Rechtslogik 1 (1974) p. 131 f. and Preface to Modern Logic in the Service of Law (1978); see more carefully *Christiane & Ota Weinberger*, Logik, Semantik, Hermeneutik (1979) p. 96 ff., *Gerhard Otte*, Zum Problem der Rechtsgeltung der juristischen Logik, Rechtstheorie (1979) p. 261 f. *Hans Kelsen*, Allgemeine Theorie der Normen, l.c. (note 2) p. 216 ff.

15) *Stig Jørgensen*, Legal Positivism and Natural Law, Values in Law, l.c. (note 8) p. 103 ff. and 29 ff.

16) General Theory of Law and State, l.c. (note 1) p. 117, 396, 437.

17) Allgemeine Theorie der Normen, l.c. (note 14) p. 206 f.

18) Ideological ideas and the actual existence (»Geltung«) respectively, On Law and Justice (1958) p. 70 ff.

19) The Concept of Law (1961) p. 97 f.

20) Thus it is wrong when *Nils Kristian Sundby* and *Torstein Eckhoff* in The Notion of Basic Norms in Jurisprudence, Scandinavian Studies in Law (1975) p. 123 ff., want to interpret the »basic norm« as the general accept of the population of the legal system. The category »duty« is here confused with its »reasons« or »genesis«.

21) See also *A. Wilson*, The Imperative Fallacy in Kelsen's Theory, in The Modern Law Review, vol. 44, 1981, 270 ff. Wilson also draws attention to the fact that Kelsen does not always maintain that the »basic norm« is a *necessary*« condition of the validity of the legal system, and so the theory collapses.

22) Concept of Law, l.c. (note 19) p. 97.

23) *Stig Jørgensen*, Recht und Gesellschaft, l.c. (note 8) p. 111 ff., *same*, Vertrag und Recht, l.c. (note 6) p. 118 ff., *same*, Values in Law, l.c. (note 8) p. 174 f.

24) *Stig Jørgensen*, Kontraktsret I (1971) p. 118 ff., *same*, Kontraktsret II (1972) p. 6 f., *same*, Erstatningsret, 2nd ed. (1972) p. 45 ff. It is Herbert Hart who has framed the idea of »defeasibility« as a part of his theory about the open character of the language. According to this conception the ideas have a general meaning, but they are subject to limitations of various kinds and in various situations, see *H. L. A. Harts*, The Ascription of Responsibility and Rights. Logic and Language, 1st Series, Oxford 1952, Ed. A. Flew. Hart has later on (the preface of Punishment and Responsibility, 1968) dissociated himself from the other idea (»ascription«) which is used in the article, but apparently not from »defeasibility«; see also *Stig Jørgensen*, Typologie und Realismus, l.c. (note 9) about the relationship between the universal and the idea of type. The former is clearly defined by means of a definite number of elements in a definite structure whereas the latter is characterized by an indefinite number of elements in a not clearly defined structure; as an example of the universal the idea of »square« may be mentioned, and as an example of the latter, the idea of »forest«. The universal may therefore form the basis of deductive conclusions on the basis of »identity« whereas the idea of type forms the basis of conclusions by analogy on the basis of »similarity«.

25) *Hans Kelsen*, General Theory, l.c. (note 1) p. 118). See *J. W. Harris*, When and Why does the Grundnorm Change?, Cambridge Law Journal 29 (1971) p. 103 ff., see also *Ojo Abiola*, The Search for a Grundnorm in Nigeria, International and Comparative Law Quaterly (1971) p. 117 ff.

26) Privy Council in Madzimbamuto, D. W. Lardner-Burke (1969) A.C. p. 645; see also *A. M. Honoré*, Reflections on Revolutions, Irish Jurist (1967) p. 268, *R. W. A. Dias*, Legal Politics. Norms behind the Grundnorm, Cambridge Law Journal 26 (1968) p. 233.

27) *Hans Kelsen*, General Theory, l.c. (note 1) p. 15 ff., *same*, The Pure Theory of Law (1967) p. 33 ff., 50 ff., 108 ff.

28) Law and Justice, l.c. (note 4) p. 70 ff., 34 ff., 53 ff., see also *Stanley Paulson*, Material and Formal Authorisation in Kelsen's Pure Theory, Cambridge Law Journal 39 (1980) p. 172 ff. and *Åke Frändberg*, Die Skandinavische Reaktion auf Hans Kelsens Reine Rechtslehre. Der Einfluss der Reine Rechtslehre auf die Rechtstheorie in verschiedenen Ländern (1978) p. 86 f.

29) *Stig Jørgensen*, Norm und Wirklichkeit, Rechtstheorie 2 (1971), p. 1 ff., and *P. M. S. Hacker*, in Hart's Philosophy of Law, in: Law, Morality and Society, Essays in Honour of H. L. A. Hart, Eds. P. M. S. Hacker and J. Raz (1977) p. 6 and 11.

30) See *Stig Jørgensen*, Norm und Wirklichkeit, l.c. (note 9) p. 1 ff. (2-3), *Ota Weinberger*, Rechtstheorie (1980) p. 427 ff.

The Criteria of Quality in Legal Science

I. The Purpose of Science

The word »quality« has entered the Danish language through German or French from the Latin »qualitas« derived from »qualis«, i.e. some sort of condition according to Greek π ο ι ο τ η σ derived from π ο ι ο σ (π ο ι) with the basic meaning, (i.e. to somewhere) heading for some place.

The lexical meaning of the word »quality« is in fact: nature, characteristic, value. So »quality« is referring to the objective characteristics of things such as weight, colour, shape, etc. which can be proved as well as to the values which are not referring to the provable characteristics of things, but to the estimating person's feelings, attitudes and purposes of the thing. When we talk about »criteria of quality«, we use the meaning last mentioned as expedient.

It is clear that an activity, including science, cannot be expedient or suitable without a purpose or an intention. A human activity without a motive is just as meaningless as an effect without a cause, says Schopenhauer. Actions must be defined as acts of will as opposed to spontaneous and mechanically enforced movements. But the motive need not be conscious since the act of will may have been provoked by an unconscious purpose.

This necessary restraint of purpose of an activity is also indicated in the word »method« which derives from the Greek μ ε τα ο δ ο σ, i.e. the way by which (one reaches the goal). Scientific method is thus the criteria which must be fulfilled in order to be able to talk about a scientific activity.

What is the purpose of science then? And what is the purpose of legal science? As regards the first question it is not possible to get much closer than to state, in general, that the purpose must be to increase our knowledge. It must be the way = the method which delimits science from other ways by which we can increase our knowledge. As opposed to the unsystematic and concrete collection of facts, science is a *systematic* activity which *generalizes* its observations in accordance with certain universals. The very first Greek science expressed its thoughts poetically by referring to the wish of finding the eternal in the changeable.

38

But what is science? What does it mean that we know something, and that we do not only wish or believe something? By this we presuppose the concept of »truth«, since true knowledge is knowledge achieved by certain methods which can be checked and reproduced.

II. Idealism and Realism in Science[1]

In this connection two very different theories of cognition can be used: speculation and empiricism. The *rationalistic* and *idealistic* sciences take their starting point in the human thought since they from some fundamental assumptions about the state of things are *deducing* their cognition which so to speak is *projected* out into the reality which is then constituted. The *empiric* (realistic) science presumes that reality already exists so that the essential thing is to describe the reality which is *reflected* by the human consciousness.

Thus the former theory of cognition is called the theory of projection achieving the maximum security by keeping itself within a well-defined system of thought and language; on the other hand, »truth«, i.e. the accordance between reality and consciousness, is doubtful. An empiric (realistic) science gives, on the contrary, a much larger accordance between reality and consciousness, whereas the security on the other hand is less, since it has been a generally accepted principle ever since David Hume's and Immanuel Kant's criticism of cognition at the end of the 18th century that you cannot infer concrete observations from general legalities. In the same way you cannot infer a cognition from a valuation.

During the latest generation the general theory of language and science has emphasized the dilemma by referring to the *autonomic* character of the language as being separated from the reality it is to describe. One of the consequences of this knowledge has been drawn from the *theory of coherence* which maintains that scientific statements can only be *verified* or *falsified* (made true or false) with reference to rules of correct language usage. The *theory of correspondence* has on the contrary maintained that it is both necessary and possible to relate reality to a statement, i.e. to verify or falsify the statement with reference to phenomena of reality.

III. Alf Ross' Realistic Legal Science[2]

Logical positivism wrongly assumed that reality so to speak reflected itself in the consciousness and was thereby transformed into a linguistic expression which could immediately be compared to reality in accordance with certain criteria of measurement. As far as legal science is concerned, *Alf Ross* would point out a »*common judge's ideology*« as the criteria of law, for which reason he referred to the grounds of legal decisions as being the actual expression of the ideology. The criterion of the truth in a statement about »existing Danish law« therefore had to be the probability of the fact that the courts in a hypothetical case, where the rule of law in question was tried, would arrive at a conclusion that was in accordance with the contents of the sentence.

There are many uncertain elements in this theory. In the first place it is not possible to prove the existence of a »common judge's ideology« which like »justice« and »the general sense of justice« - which Alf Ross rejects as being unscientific metaphysics - is a statement about the existence of a common legal ideology for all judges; the very existence of dissents and contradictory judgments demonstrates this fact. Secondly these »prognoses«, i.e. statements of legal science about future probable expressions of the judge's ideology, are at the same time a *source of law*. Thus the doctrine is not only partly self-verifying and like other social scientific prognoses part of the consciousness that is described, but it is also *prescribing* as far as the doctrine is recognized as a legal source which it is expressly assumed to be in modern legal practice.

Nor is it realistic to assume that legal science in fact makes this kind of calculation of probability. It is not only uncertain which probability is sufficient, but this probability is by legal science based on an immediate description and interpretation of the existing source of law material in accordance with »the legal method« which the scientist masters just as well as the judges. In fact »the theory of prognosis« is inspired by the Anglo-Saxon - especially the American - idea of law where the judges are legal notabilities.

In addition to this Alf Ross had to regard both interpretations of the source of law material and the judicial decision itself as an evaluating process in accordance with his theory of legal science. Thus large parts of the dogmatic legal science (de sententia ferenda) became politics while the judicial decision was an actual process of motivation and the grounds a later »facade legitimation«. The former consequence was serious enough since the greater part of legal science - the interpreting part - became unscientific; the latter was fatal since the only source of information of knowledge about »existing Danish law«, viz. the judges' feelings of what they are obliged to do is in principle uncertain.

The decisive weakness in Ross' legal theory, which also applies to the so-called »Scandinavian realism« (or »the Uppsala School«), is, however, the presumption that law must be understood as a »phenomenon of reality« in the external world, i.e. either as behaviour or ideology by which legal science turns into sociology or psychology. By this legal science prevents itself from describing and interpreting an authoritative set of rules, or in other words the legal *norms*.

IV. Legal Science as Interpreting Science[3]

By reducing our visual field to *»existing law«* in that (empirical) sense by stressing the *judges'* conception of law you prevent yourself *from* describing and interpreting the norms which have *validly* become a part of Danish law according to the principles of the sources of law - however, without being part of the judges' consciousness - and you prevent yourself *from* criticizing the judgments and the grounds for the judgments which are in fact realized. The content of the principles of the sources of law concerning the criteria of how valid Danish law comes into existence is a historical and cultural matter.

It is easy enough to refer to the rules of the existing constitution concerning the formation of statutes. This is, however, not sufficient at all since other forms of material are recognized as legal (e.g. customary law, court practice, legal science) just as there is an extensive *consensus* among the jurists concerning which arguments are recognized as legal (de sententia ferenda, i.e. advice to the judges and other people solving conflicts) and which are political (de lege ferenda, i.e. advice to the legislature). In the Danish so-called »Christiania case« the Supreme Court thus rejected the reference of the High Court saying that »the free city« was a »social experiment« and therefore a matter of Parliament which ironically enough had referred the case to the courts of law, (Ugeskrift for Retsvæsen (U) 1978.315), and in a comment on a judgment of the Supreme Court in U 1984.284 (U 1984. B.49) it is said that an objective tort liability for damages demands statutory authority.

It is clear that such rules of valid legal argumentation exist, but on the other hand it is difficult to state their contents in a few words, among other things because they are different in different branches of law which are controlled by different legal principles and ideas. Among other things, criminal law is controlled by the principle of legality, while the law of bankruptcy is dominated by the principle of equality, public law by competing considerations of security and efficiency, the law of procedure by the principle of contradiction, and private law by the principle of equivalence. Since the purpose of the rules of law is to regulate the behaviour in society, both considerations of purpose and of consequence play an essential part in the complicated set of rules of interpretation and argumentation which has developed through the ages.

By this we have already demonstrated the very decisive weakness of the *logico-empirical* theory of science: The belief that language and reality are immediately comparable or in other words that the description can be objective. It was the *analytic* and *hermeneutic* philosophy of language that drew attention to the *intentional* character of the language which resulted in the fact that any description of reality necessarily implicates an evaluation in the form of an interpretation and a qualification of reality in connection with the system of language.

Therefore, when you deal with criteria of quality in legal science it is very important to understand that the object of legal science is not to make objective descriptions of phenomena of reality, but to *interpret* an *authoritative normative* material with the *purpose* of the norms as a basis. The purposes of these norms are to regulate the social behaviour in accordance with a set of cultural and political ideas and with an evaluation of the *consequences* of the different possibilities of interpretation and their accordance with the *purpose* or purposes.

V. The Principles of Reality and Rationality[4]

The *dogmatic* legal science does therefore, in principle, not differ from the application of the law. Both activities deal with the solution of legal disputes. The practician solves real conflicts whereas the theorist takes a decision on hypothetic conflicts; the practician *must* arrive at a decision whereas the theorist *can* let the solution of a problem remain unsettled; the practician must probably consider if his decision is consistent with earlier and later decisions in accordance with »the nature of things« whereas it is the theorist's main object to adapt his solutions of the problems to systematic considerations which express the general ideas and principles of the branch of law and aim at a *consistency* in accordance with the principle of rationality.

The principle of rationality must necessarily be a superior principle in legal science as it has been ever since the Glossatores in the Bolognian Middle Ages for the first time tried to bring consistency and coherence into the traditional, outmoded, and diffuse but authoritative (Roman) source material. If the principle of rationality must be a superior principle in legal science it is not only because the method of science as mentioned above, in general, must be systematic and generalizing, but because the *principle of justice* in the sense: that equal cases are treated equally, is another way of expressing the conception of rule. That equal cases are treated equally means that they must be treated in accordance with a rule. The *formal justice* demands rules which enable man to predict the behaviour of others and by that the consequences of his own actions. The *material justice* depends on the contents of the rules which again *partly* depend on the special ideas within the individual branch of law, *partly* on the existing cultural and political situation.

But legal science must not only respect the principle of rationality but must also recognize the *principle of reality*. This means that the legal scientist must know the purpose and the function of the conditions of life in question - since it is the purpose of the rules to regulate certain conditions of life - as mentioned above

- and it is therefore impossible to interpret the rules without knowledge of that reality.

However, the legal scientist cannot be content with having knowledge of a special part of life. If the scientist shall be able to fit his branch into a larger systematic connection, he must have a superior knowledge not only of the *whole legal system*, but also of the *social conditions* in general.

The person who deals with labour law must for instance be familiar with the entire law of contracts in order to fit the solutions of the problems concerning labour law into a perspective of the general law of contracts. Much insecurity and ambiguity in the special law of contracts, especially the part which has been subjected to a political administrative process of control, such as the law of tenancy, the law of employment, etc., are due to the fact that the law of contracts has been left to specialists who have not kept the connection to the general system of law. The same applies to other branches of law such as the law of taxation, company law, and environmental law in the widest sense.

That the systematic connection must be corrected in consideration of the *development of society* is another aspect. The general idea of private law based on the principle of will and freedom counteracts the modern idea of the *Welfare-State* which modifies the principle of will not only with the interest of commerce and the principle of objective interpretation, but also with the principle of equality and the society's protection of those who are in a weak strategic position. The development of labour law is an example of the fact that actions, which are normally illegal, are accepted in certain respects when by means of collective force the purpose is to protect the weak wage earners.

New branches of law detached from the traditional systematism have therefore arisen: environmental law and business law, including consumer purchases, company law, maritime law, and law of tenancy with elements of both private law and public law. Labour law arose as a completely new branch of law during the first third of this century.

From the principle of rationality and reality follows that the mutual inspiration between theory and *legal practice* is essential for the adaptation. Practice provides theory with information about the practical solutions of problems, and theory provides practice with an analysis and a criticism of the adaptation of the individual decisions to a general system of law and ideas.

VI. Legal Method[5]

In the society of today the knowledge of the legislation and administrative regulations must, of course, be the primary basis of dogmatics since this production of rules in the Constitution is stated as the primary source of law which *must* form the basis of the legal decision. Besides, no definite rules concerning the priority of the remaining *source material* which *may* be quoted can be stated perhaps apart from the fact that Supreme Court judgments have a high priority.

Neither are there any established rules which indicate to what extent the preparatory work of statutes is decisive for the construction of the purpose of the law. It is not correct either to ascribe the purpose of the law the decisive impact on interpretation. Among other things it is possible that the purpose cannot be achieved through the rules of law.

However, the purpose must respect the linguistic *word border*, unless it is shown that there is a *mistake* in the process of legislation which has happened now and then. *Systematism* and other *logical* considerations must be respected as well. On the other hand it must be borne in mind that conclusions by analogy and contrast are normally logical methods of conclusions, but in reality an evaluation of whether a rule of law is exhaustive or not, and that different rules of presumption apply to different branches of law. While conclusions by analogy as a principal rule are excluded in criminal law out of consideration for the legal security they are as a general rule allowed in the law of contract, at least as far as the relationship between the parties is concerned.

Thus the criteria of quality of legal science partly coincide with the criteria of the identification and interpretation of the existing source of law material in the so-called *»legal method«*.

As *Knud Illum* once said, it is not possible to describe the method exhaustively, it has to be learned through legal training, *partly* through the legal education *partly* through legal practice. An important distinction is here the argumentation *de sententia ferenda* and *de lege ferenda*. As stated above the dogmatic legal science gives good advice to the courts and administrative institutions concerning which possibilities of interpretation to prefer among the possibilities being compatible with the linguistic content of the norm. The recommendation must, of course, respect the systematic, teleological and pragmatic regards which must be stated and discussed. General references to »expediency« or »practical« considerations« are *partly* meaningless *partly* a necessary cover for one's own inarticulate estimates.

It is the so-called »critical science« which in the strongest way has emphasized the demand for an open argumentation on account of the possibility of criticism and discussion of the decisions made, including hypothetical proposals of solutions of problems in legal science. But it is a general moral philosophic assumption that the real reasons for a decision must be stated openly whereas the person who decides in return has a claim to be taken at his word and not suspected of justifying his decisions with false arguments such as the American and

Scandinavian realism have claimed supported by certain elements of the »critical legal science«, especially the Marxian one.

The decisive thing is therefore to know which arguments are recognized as legal, remaining within the framework of the politico-juridical system, and which arguments are going beyond this and then become political. Or, in other words, where is the borderline between the solutions that the judges may choose without legislation and the solutions demanding legislation. Above the so-called »Christiania case« and another case are mentioned in which the Supreme Court decided on that subject.

We have to keep our legal argumentation within this very indistinct framework since we in our community, governed by law, must recognize the devision of functions among the different institutions of the community. Judges are not like politicians elected by the people and have therefore no political authority to make political decisions. But because of the crisis of the democracies during the latest 10-15 years there has been a general tendency, however, to »classify« political problems, which the political system cannot manage, for instance the above »Christiania-case«, cases concerning boycotts, cases concerning the environment, etc., as »legal«. The reluctance of the courts of law to get themselves involved in political cases is understandable and respectable since the courts of law otherwise would lose their reliability as impartial conflict solvers.

VII. Conclusion

I have now reached the end. And many might think that it was not far. The »realistic« legal science was apparently far more scientific and had some clear criteria of quality. It was so very simple to refer to »the objective description« and »the mechanism of verification« of natural science. But in that way legal science shirked the responsibility of its opinions and referred instead to the probability of the judges' having this opinion.

As mentioned above it is, however, only a seeming security and clarity. Speaking about others' interpretations of the source of law material is, as mentioned, only a superfluous evasion, which does not throw light on anything, but on the contrary exempts legal science from its duty to state its own arguments. It is on the manner that this duty is fulfilled that the quality of legal science shall be judged.

Notes
1) *Stig Jørgensen*, Values in Law (1978) p. 29 ff.
2) See below p. 87.

3) Stig Jørgensen, Pluralis Juris (1982) p. 41 ff. with note 70.
4) Pluralis Juris (1.c. note 3) p. 7 and 14 ff. Values in Law (1.c. note 1) p. 59.
5) See below p. 47 f.

Motive and Justification
in Legal Decision-Making[1]

I. Judicial Decision

In consequence of its behaviouristic foundation *American* realism had to reject the existence of special sources of law and instead consider the judicial decision as a stimulus-response relation. The most extreme consequence of this is the so-called »digestion-theory«: all elements of motivation, including the judge's breakfast and its influence on his mood, are relevant as »sources of law«, i.e. motives of the judicial decision. Thus legal science turns into sociology and psychology.

Conversely, the *Continental* legal theory has from different philosophical basic views emphasized the normative nature of law and the judicial decision. The Kantian distinction between *sein* and *sollen* has in all essentials been accepted as the foundation of legal obligation. The distinction between »the realm of necessity«, i.e. the physical world presupposing the law of causation, and the »realm of freedom«, i.e. the world of action presupposing responsibility and thus the freedom of will, splits up cognition into *theoretical* cognition and *practical* cognition. Theoretical cognition is about the »right« organization of the physical world, practical cognition is about the »right« action.

In this century logical empiricism has revived this distinction and maintained that only statements have *meaning*, as the meaning of a statement is identical with its conditions of truth, i.e. the criteria laid down in advance either in the form of conceptual definitions or a set of measuring instruments. Only such analytical or synthetical sentences referring either to logico-mathematical deductive systems or to measutable sides of reality can have meaning as they can be either true or false. On the other hand metaphysical or evaluating statements are without meaning as they have no criteria of truth.

The criticism of positivism has since tried to bridge this fundamental distinction between theoretical and practical cognition. Indeed it would be unsatisfactory if there was no difference between rational and irrational valuations and actions. On the one hand it is realized that no cognition is »objective« as it has to be described in an ordinary language and that this language qualification implies an infinite number of choices, as real phenomena have to to be fitted into a mentally created conceptual system. On the other hand valuations are only to a limited extent completely subjective, as it is possible to come to more or less intersubjective agreement about an action's being right or wrong, if its purposes and effects are adequately clarified.

Some people go so far as to assume that there is no *fundamental* difference between cognition and valuation, but only a quantitative difference of the defining of relevant criteria. I am not convinced about the correctness of this argument, there may, however, be reasonable grounds for building a linguistic bridge between the two categories of statement. Thus by the word *meaning* can be understood *an assumption or a belief* that certain matters of fact are present or that a certain conduct is the correct one. If we want to be taken seriously as rationally thinking individuals, we must, however, be prepared and able to give *reasons* for this belief. We must not forget *that* these reasons or motives for our actions are often firmly anchored in attitudes, outlooks, needs and ideas, which are deeply rooted in our nature and culture, and *that* our description of reality usually must be made not with certainty but with different degrees of probability. Obviously these factors based on feelings and uncertainty limit the certainty of our argumentation. Ideological criticism has wanted to disclose discrepancies between the formal grounds for an action and the real motives. *Legitimation* and *justification* are the expressions used as extenuative motives; and adducing extenuative motives is claimed to be universal in any case in repressive societies. On the other hand, moral philosophy has warned against throwing suspicion on human motives as does ideological criticism. Instead *K. E. Løgstrup* demands that the agent is to be taken at his word when he states his grounds.

The so-called *Scandinavian realism* in jurisprudence has indeed stressed the law as a real phenomenon but it does not reject the existence of a legal *obligation*; on the contrary it has considered positive law to be the only real law in contrast to different forms of natural law. *Alf Ross* conceives in principle law as an ideology which the judge regards as binding. On the other hand this ideology is only expressed authoritatively by the judge in his references to the rules of law, which he states in the grounds for his decisions. Thus law is a real phenomenon and is therefore of importance only as *»existing law«*, i.e. the rules of law, which are actually applied, as they are stated in the grounds of a judicial decision.

On the other hand Alf Ross adopts the logico-empiric assumption that valuations are in principle irrational. The motives of any decision, including the judicial decision, avoid rational control, and the grounds for the decision will therefore be pseudo-grounds. It seems to be difficult to maintain at a time that the premises of a judgement offer the only possible way of obtaining an insight in existing law and that one cannot be sure whether these premises are true, as the judge may in fact be motivated by other purposes or considerations. However, logically it may be possible to assume that the judge actually refers to the normative material, by which he feels bound, and which he thinks that others will accept too as a sufficient justification of his decision, even if it is not his real motives.

The crux of the matter is, however, that Ross in principle presupposes the existence of a material, by which the judge feels legally bound. The difficulties arise especially because he chooses as his starting point the situation of the judge or the administration, which is at best an unnecessary circumlocution. As *Knud Illum* puts it, the judge's possibility of obtaining an insight in the legally binding material is the same as that of other jurists, for also the judges take their ideology from sources which they consider to be binding. Otherwise the judge would have to make his decisions from his own perception of the obligation and he would not be told where to find information about what is binding for him and others.

Similarly *Herbert Hart* has rejected descriptive definitions of law and considers it important to distinguish between cause and obligation. On the other hand to him the obligation is nothing but a logical category and not as to Ross a sociological or psychological phenomenon. So while Ross is interested in the *reality* of the law, Hart as well as *Hans Kelsen* regard the *validity* of the law as the crucial problem. Like *Immanuel Kant*, Kelsen looked upon the norms as imperatives belonging not to the world of reality but to the world of freedom, which means that they cannot be justified by referring to physical causes, but only by referring to a higher norm in a system ending with a »basic norm«. Hart derives law from the rules of recognition which indicate the actual criteria for the valid production of rules of law of a given society; in primitive societies it is especially custom, in developed societies especially statutes, regulations and other authoritatively produced written material.

Most countries (but not Great Britain) have a written constitution stating the most important criteria for the production of rules of law.

Also other material than statutes, etc., custom and legal usage can be classified as legal material in the sense that it can form part of the grounds for a judgement. We see, how references to the *motives* of laws, their *objects* and *consequences* form part of the *interpretation of the law*. Also references to the *legal doctrine*, the dogmatic legal science, have been used in recent Danish legal practice. However, also certain *legal patterns of argumentation* have through the ages been recognized as parts of the legal tradition offering a certain technique among other things by filling in a gap in the law in the form of *conclusions by analogy* or *extended interpretation*, or conversely in the form of *conclusions by contrast* and *restricted interpretation*. It is an obvious fact that these figures are used when adapting the law to changed or un-noticed social conditions, however, the decision which figure to choose is governed by pragmatic considerations. The figures state how far you may go as regards legal changes without legislation.

The Danish constitution lays down a rank-order relation among the most important sources of law: laws, regulations, decrees, etc., but not between laws and other sources of law and between one statute and the other. According to our constitution the courts, of course, cannot pass judgements in defiance of the law, but the relation between law and custom and between the other sources of law and legal argumentation is undetermined. However, as regards statutes the general principle is that *new* statutes have priority over older ones and that *special* statutes have priority over general ones. However, it is not a certain rule of priority as it may be broken by other considerations, e.g. by information about (probable) errors in the legislative procedure.

However, further arguments are accepted by the application of law. References to *justice* and *equity* occur in the legislation, but even without authority in statutes such references occur in legal usage. From time immemorial *equality* and *reciprocity* have been crucial reasons of justice, while *reasons of equity* have been an important means for a reasonable application of general rules in concrete cases.

It is no mere coincidence that *Viggo Bentzon* has said about »the nature of things«, the most subsidiary »source of law«, that it prompts a decision which combines the regard for settling the case according to a general rule with the consideration for concrete justice. By this we have arrived at the sum of *legal ideas* and *social considerations* which have evolved and underlie our European and Nordic culture. This background of political, religious and cultural values underlying our socio-liberal democracies is sometimes - like in the German Federal Republic and in the U.S.A. - more or less explicitly indicated in the constitutions, but even beside that it is indispensable that we in our argumentation of a judicial decision take as our starting point *the general consensus* in society.

There is reason for the belief that the cases causing special problems of argumentation are the *atypical* cases (hard cases), whereas the uncomplicated cases are settled on the basis of consensus about the fundamental attitude in the field in question.

The basis of argumentation is for instance not the same within *criminal law* as within *private law*. While conclusions by analogy as a rule are out of the question in the first-mentioned cases, as the criminal law is presumed to be exhaustive, conclusions by analogy and extended interpretation and other more free patterns of argumentation are widespread within private law, which only to a limited extent has been regulated by detailed legislation. If there is a legislation it will often be of a general and abstract nature supplemented by omnibus clauses (cf. the Danish Contracts Act § 36), thus leaving the detailed regulation to private autonomy.

An exception from this situation - in fact with increasing importance - is the special legislation within private law, which out of political regards is to regulate the rights and obligations of the parties to one another. An example of this is the housing legislation in the widest sense, which is also amply represented in my material. In these fields the frequent legislative initiatives will often result in incomplete and unco-ordinated regulations, which may now and then conceal a deliberate confusion in the political process, which refers a political disagreement to be settled by the courts.

Public law will to a higher extent be influenced by *political regards* on the one hand and by regards for *the rule of law* on the other hand. Therefore, in these cases there will often be references to law motives and to equity and justice. *The law of legal procedure* is exceptional in so far as the object of the procedure is to secure *consideration of justice* through the basic principle of civil procedure: *audiatur et altera pars*, and through the principles of criminal procedure: *the burden of proof* of the Prosecution and *the principle of public trial*.

Thus it is a fact that there is a legal tradition in the widest sense which has arisen within the history of law, legal science and rhetoric along with the Western socio-liberal cultural tradition. Add to this a special Nordic and Danish political, cultural and legal tradition, which at any rate during the last 150 years has been characterized by an interplay of theory and practice and an explicit recognition of *utilitarian* and *pragmatic* arguments.

However, the argumentation of the courts still show the traces of their primary function, which is to administer existing law, but no doubt the courts still make new law and develop existing law by their practice as abstract rules are concretized by their application.

For an existentialist legal theory this view is intensified to its utter consequence, as it is maintained that law is not established until it is concretized; so far it exists only as a possibility.

Anyhow it is important to emphasize the *objective* element in the application of the law: it is the law and not the judge which makes the decision. In fact this is the basic principle of the constitutional state. In its written form the decision appears as a *logical conclusion*. On the other hand it cannot be denied that the judicial decision in principle is a *decision* implying estimates in several fields, which can be divided analytically in the following way, although in practice it is an undivisible or *dialectical* process of thought.

1. In most of the questionable cases it will be possible to apply several different rules which may lead to different results. (*Choice of rules*).
2. By the interpretation of the existing rules not only the wording of the written material, i.e. the *lexical* (linguistic) meaning, is to be taken into consideration, but also the *systematic* (logical) placing of the rules in the law or the legislation, as well as the motives concerning the *objects* of the rule (teleological/historical) and its *consequences* (pragmatic). The object of rules of law is actually to influence and control reality. (Choice of legal considerations).
3. Also by the selection of the facts, which are considered to be relevant, is made an estimated valuation which is a consequence of the same considerations about the objects of the rules and the means by which to achieve them including their desirable consequences related to legal, moral and political ideas and principles. (*Choice of facts*).

Several legal *tricks* aim, as mentioned, at pushing the estimative element into the background (conclusions by analogy and by contrast, lex specialis, superior and posterior). It is of value to state such limits to the legal estimate in the judicial decision. However, to promote clarity and the rule of law it is important to point out the real argumentation in the decision, as it will then be easier to accept the decision, even for the loser, and at any rate it will offer the best foundation for criticism of the decision in the form of appeal. In fact the demand for justification implies the demand for an open argumentation.

Just as I must repudiate a monistic jurisprudence[2] and doctrine of rights[3], I must accept a pluralistic source-of-law-theory. To legal psychology and legal sociology it is of great importance to examine judges' and administrators' motivation in the widest sense: their cultural, ideological and political views and their personal and economic-social attitudes to the different types of conflicts and groups of persons. The justification of a judicial decision is most important for legal dogmatics and legal philosophy. A descriptive source-of-law-theory is most important for advocates, who have to isolate the arguments, which are actually stated as the grounds for a judicial decision, in anticipation of producing a convincing material for criticism of a concrete case (appeal) or in support of a similar case. Thus it is the advocates who are most interested in reading the judges' comments on their decisions. But also judges, administrators and dogmatic legal scientists have naturally taken an interest in the grounds for the judgements.

However, from a legal philosophical point of view it is indisputable that a descriptive source-of-law-theory does not solve the problem of the source of law. Anyhow when judges have to arrive at a decision and consequently offer an opinion on how a certain case is to be settled it is not sufficient to refer to how they usually justify their judgements. Also from a dogmatic scientific point of view it must be presupposed that a certain legal material is prescribing when it has been duly established according to a given society's rules of how to make binding rules of law (rules of recognition).

Nevertheless I find that the analysis of the argumentation and justification of the judicial decision is of the utmost importance, as it gives an insight in the types of cases giving rise to difficult legal conflicts at a given time as well as the arguments which the judge and administrator consider valid and convincing as grounds to the parties and the surrounding society. It must be borne in mind that the machinery of justice only deals with social problems which have not been assimilated by society as a whole or by individual groups or persons.

The main object af legal argumentation is then to adapt an atypical conflict material to the generally accepted social consensus. This consensus as well as the appropriate argumentation for the adaption of the conflict material to the consensus change and must necessarily change along with the development of the conditions of the surrounding society.

New legal arguments are accepted; nowadays there is an open recognition of *pragmatic* argumentation, and references to legal *theory* and *legal practice* appear in the grounds for the judgment instead of just appearing in the editorial notes. It is interesting that »*the nature of things*«, which refers to the »natural« arrangement of the conditions of life, and which through centuries has been used by the source -of-law-theory, in recent legal decisions has been replaced by direct references to *legal valuation* of these conditions: »reasonable«, »just«, »equitable«, »common sense«, etc.

Although there is a tendency to make direct references to supplementary *normative material*, such as regulations, circulars, guidelines, usage, etc., there is as well an increasing tendency -especially in fields being subject to a violent process of change - to look for the political aims of this (i.e. normative material) in *the motives* of the statutes.

Indeed, it is suggestive that the large majority of judicial decisions, which openly discuss legal argumentation, concerns the understanding and consequently the application of the administrative protective legislation of *public law* and *private law*.

Thus the source-of-law-doctrine cannot be static, but has *dynamically* to adapt itself to the social and legal tendencies in society. Like Niklas Luhman you may say that it reflects the development from the liberal to the welfare state.

The material, on which my article was based, consisted of legal decisions of the Danish high courts and Supreme Court from the years 1975-1979. A recent - not yet published follow-up analysis of the subsequent five years' court practice shows the same dynamic picture with an even further developed open argumentation in the grounds.

Notes

1) See Stig Jørgensen's analysis of Danish legal practice, in: Die rechtliche Entscheidung und ihre Begründung, Rhetorische Rechtstheorie, Ed. O. Ballweg und Th. M. Seibert (1982) p. 337.
2) *Stig Jørgensen*, Pluralis Juris, Acta Jutlandica (1982).
3) *Stig Jørgensen*, Private Property, Gedächtnisschrift für Ilmar Tammelo (1984) p. 615.

Effectiveness and Morality

Navigare necesse est
vivere non est necesse
Pompeius

I. Introduction

The word »morality« is, like the word »ethics«, derived from respectively the Latin and the Greek word for »custom« and refers to the correspondence of an act with the socially recognized rules, whereas »effectiveness« refers to its ability to produce the desired consequences. Science develops *methods*, i.e. roads, by which one obtains good results.

Now effectiveness and expediency are words, which are meaningless, as far as no aim or purpose is proposed. The theory of science decides which methods science must apply, but if effectiveness is made *the aim* itself it stops to be science and turns into »scientism«.

The debate within philosophy of science has at times blurred the delimination between aims and means. Positivism has at times taken a form which presupposes an instrumental conception of man, i.e. that man is conceived as a means, whereas the so-called »critical science«, derived from an ontology (assumption as to the essence of man), turns science into a political means.

II. Behaviourism

The American psychologist *B. F. Skinner* dramatically emphasized the moral philosophical dilemma when he in his book raised the question of whether modern society can afford freedom.[1] Skinner is with his good or bad qualities identified with behaviouristic psychology which regards man instrumentally, i.e. as a means, and not teleologically, i.e. as a goal. According to the first conception the aim of psychology is not to analyse the technological, economical and political evolution but to adapt the individual to the existing society. According to the second conception the aim of psychology primarily is to analyse the demands of human beings, or put in another way: What is the essence of man (ontology)?

The behaviouristic psychology is often identified with the experiments with rats which dealt with the relations between *stimulus* and response and proved that rats could learn rather complicated forms of behaviour by different stimulations. Of course there is nothing wrong about measuring and describing the reactions of animals and human beings to external actions, just as there is nothing wrong about registrating and describing physiological processes of human beings and their interaction with the surroundings and about the study of children's development and adaptation to the existing society. The *principle of reality* demands that science takes as its starting point the existing reality when analysing concepts as sickness and education, and not a hypothetical future society.

The mistake of behaviourism is not that it takes its issue from the interaction of man with the existing reality, but that it turns science into philosophy or ideology and even politics, when assuming a certain »essence« of man. When for instance Skinner puts the question whether mankind can afford freedom, the adaptation of man to society is made the goal and not the means, and behaviourism has become »scientism« or moral philosophy.[2]

What is wrong about this is that a particular methodology is made *the* scientific method and that methodology *hypostatizes* one - essential - aspect of reality and science to be the reality, which implies a presupposition of the essence of man, nature and society, and becomes ontology. All sciences know about the tendency to develop *monism*, and the history of legal science demonstrates its tendency to follow a general scientific pattern or »paradigm«.

III. History of Science

Natural science has from the days of antiquity deliminated the course of humanities and social science.[3] According to *Aristotle* all science was teleological, i.e. dependent on a particular purpose, because the analysis of the *essence* indicates which ideal the individual »thing« is aiming at and which energy or power is operating in that direction.

Social science therefore must start speculatively by defining the essence of man and his purpose and the direction of the purposive process. This philosophy of science dominates even the world picture of the Middle Ages, which was founded on the geocentric theory. The Renaissance with Galileo's refined technique of measurement turned the picture upside-down. Already in the late Middle Ages Aristotle's conceptual realism was attacked, but it was not until the heliocentric cosmology was accepted that Galileo definitely rejected the teleological approach in science and recommended that *measurement* be the fundament of science.

This Copernican turn of science was accepted by the humanities including jurisprudence, which in the 17th and 18th centuries developed the rationalistic natural law theory from Grotius and Pufendorf to Leibniz and Wolff, according to which law was conceived as eternally valid laws of nature, which permitted the finding of correct answers to legal questions entirely by intellectual cognition. Just like cosmos society was regarded as a big machinery of a clock, working according to natural laws with God as the clockmaker, who originally started the clockwork. In the case of contradiction between natural law, which was a combination of law and morals (»right«, »reasonable« laws), and positive law, positive law was in principle invalid, but in practice natural law originally functioned rather as good advice to the prince. In the late 18th century, however, it turned out to be the legitimation of the American and French revolutions.

The development of the new chemical and biological sciences in the early 19th century created a new analogy also for the legal science. The concept of movement and *process* penetrated the thinking in philosophy; *Immanuel Kant* rejected natural law and parted cognition and evaluation. He distinguished between *theoretical* and *practical* cognition. Theoretical cognition deals with the right cognition of the natural world, governed by the law of causation, the world of necessity; practical cognition deals with the theory of the right action, which belongs to the world of freedom, because responsibility is impossible without freedom of action.

Freedom was the leading idea in Kant's social philosophy, and therefore it was easy for him to accept *David Hume*'s foregoing *subjectivistic* theory of cognition based on the insight that individuals and not humanity conceive. It was a consequence of that theory that no objective cognition is possible neither in the natural nor in the moral world. Thus natural laws cannot be proved and moral statements only reflects the feelings of the cognizing person and not qualities of the things. *Kant* on his behalf accepted Hume's criticism but held that necessity of an organized cognition and of an organized society respectively *presupposed* the existence of natural law and the freedom of will. The consequential separation of natural and moral cognition opened the doors for *technical evolution* and *legal positivism*.

With *Hegel* the idealism of Kant was combined with the theory of historical *evolution* which was made the general basis of cognition. Liberty was still the first principle of society, but it was reduced to be the insight in historical necessity, which is the outcome of facts and natural laws. This theory of evolution became even more persuasive with *Darwin*'s general theory of biological evolution and led in one respect to a general belief in progress and in a reversed form to *Karl Marx'* historical materialism. While Hegel chose as his starting point the idea and its dialectical evolution in history, Marx saw society, culture and law as a reflection of the basic material conditions. The working class is according to the theory the actual dialectical opponent to the capitalists' leading history to the Communist society.

This Marxian conflict model of society was in accordance with another turn in the conception of science. Already *Schopenhauer* had emphasized that the human will is the motor of society and that an action without a motive is like an effect without a cause. The will is therefore led by *interests*, collective as well as individual. *Rudolph von Jhering* saw law as the meeting point of conflicting social interests and politics as the battle about the law. The political democracies of the late 19th and early 20th centuries drew the consequences of that situation and lost their beliefs in a *»reasonable common will«* which was the original idea of democracy.

The theory of evolution remains alive in politics, science and philosophy alongside with positivism and naturalism, which emerged with the breakdown of idealism. *Auguste Comte*, the founder of *positivism*, aimed at introducing statistics and quantitative methods into sociology, so that social processes could be treated like processes in the natural world. *Naturalism* treats individuals and society as natural phenomena, whose actions are regarded as cause and effect according to natural laws. Responsibility, of course, ceases to have any sense, and treatment is the adequate reaction to a crime. In *Sigmund Freud*'s psycho-analytical theory the concepts of good and evil vanish as a moral category.

The extreme individualism, which lies behind freudianism, is also apparent in existentialism, which *S. Kierkegaard* developed already in the middle of the 19th century, opposing the philosophical system of Hegel, in which he underpins the principle of individual responsibility. One is living forwards and understanding it backwards, Kierkegaard says; therefore, the individual must accept responsibility for his choice of possibilities in each existential situation, because the true consequences cannot be conceived until afterwards.

It was not until this century that nuclear physics and the *theory of relativity* along with the experience of World War I killed the philosophy of evolution. The new physics made it clear that cognition cannot be »objective«, as the description of the processes depends upon the measuring instruments applied, which in its turn influence the processes described. Especially for social sciences it is of significant importance that prediction of future behaviour is one of the motivating factors of that behaviour.

IV. Contemporary Theories of Science

A. Logical Empiricism

The scientific pluralism resulting from that philosophy of science tends to confirm the scientist's perception of himself being the neutral technician, who chooses the perspective and task, which are solely determined by the cognition.[4] The so-called »Wiener Circle«, logical empiricism and positivism, stressed further the perspective aiming at the value-free cognition. In order to avoid the usurpation of the powerful political and religious ideologies of the 20s and 30s, Fascism, Marxism and Catholicism, science must and must only deal with logic or »reality« which can be demonstrated and described in a presumably objective language. Metaphysical assertions and evaluations are according to that theory without sense, because no criteria are available for verification of metaphysical assertions, and evaluations are not objective but expressions of the feelings of the evaluator. The Danish legal philosopher, *Alf Ross*, consequently characterized expressions about justice as »inarticulate outbursts«, a »bang in the table«, and even worse.

B. Critical Theory

There is a certain irony about the fact that logical empiricism, the aim of which was to protect science against the ideology of the »critical theory« of the 60s, was regarded as the major enemy representing the reactionary and suppressing Capitalism. On the other hand there is nothing surprising about the fact that the ideological movement of »liberation«, which headed the attack on the liberal society, must regard an objective science as its main target. In recent years we have often witnessed how a political struggle is disguised as a discussion about the right scientific theory.

The starting signal in the West came from the so-called Frankfurter School. One of the senior members, *Th. Adorno*, coined the concept of »negativism«.[5] Where positivism would ask: How?, hermeneutics would ask: Why?, the negativist would ask: Why not? Where the positivist would describe reality as it is, the negativist would put question marks against the actual situation, which is of particular importance for the social scientist, who is dealing with the »soft« reality of society and human mind contrary to the natural scientist, who deals with the »hard« reality. Adorno actually criticized sociology for treating human beings as elements in the natural sciences, which have to be adapted to society and not vice versa according to their demands.

Herbert Marcuse went even further taking his issue from a Freudian-Marxian conception of man and its demand for liberation. In contradiction to the Platonian-romantic idea of »the complete man« he framed the concept of the »one-dimensional man« or »the technological man«, which in his capacity of working power and consumer is adapted to modern technology and its demand for efficiency and growth.

More serious was the younger *Jürgen Habermas*, who, influenced by hermeneutic philosophy and new-Hegelian rationalism - just like the English analytical philosophy of language -, pointed to the interestboundness of science as a human activity. All concepts contain elements of evaluation being abstract destillations of elements of concrete reality ordered according to our purpose and interests. A *»table«* for instance is a spherial construction with the practical purpose to put things on it, a *»wood«* is a group of trees of a certain size and density, a *»terrorist«* and a »freedom fighter« may be the same person viewed from different sides. From this correct analysis of the necessary interdependence between cognition and interest, some dramatic shortcuts were made by the followers: When objectivity is dead, subjectivity is the truth!, and: When science is not politically neutral, all science is politics!

It is obvious that such quasilogic is false. The correct conclusion must be that the evaluative and political elements of science must be isolated and expressly indicated as presuppositions of science. For instance it is today clear that selection of a project is not value-free and certainly not the priorities made by the society in its appropriations. It is equally clear that more or less *intersubjectivity* is possible concerning the relevance of the formulations of problems and the basic assumptions. Habermas himself believed in the inherent ability of reason to reach the »truth« and thereby the »right« society through a free debate, an opinion related to the idea of *Karl Popper*'s »open society«. But the Marxist ideology soon took over the leadership of the »critical theory«, which was turned into a rigid »capital-logical« analysis, whose purpose was to justify the necessity of transition of society into Communism.

The circle was now closed, and the ideology-criticism of positivism was turned into the killing of positivism by the new ideology-criticism. The »established« science was not blameless itself. Many scientists were not able to cope with a philosophical debate, other found such debates superfluous and still others were convinced that science and politics should be kept apart.

V. Effectiveness and Morality

When we now turn to the initial question about affording freedom, it is obvious that the question is put in accordance with the criticizable »scientism«. Science cannot decide how social values shall be distributed, and not presuppose that material values are more important than immaterial values, and that economic growth comes before freedom and justice. We must step up at the higher level of metascience, not the first one of philosophy of science, but the second one of ethics of science or moral philosophy.

The *pluralistic* philosophy of science, which I find convincingly right,[6] accepts that different problems demand the use of different methods, but when the »political« choice of project has been made and the concepts and interests involved have been analysed, one must respect the necessity of »objective« quantitative methods and their relevance in social sciences.[7] The counting must be relevant and correctly made even in those sciences.

Ergo, it is not the task of science to make priorities between economy and liberty. On the other hand economy can of course tell us about the prize of liberty, but the final decision lies at the moral and political level.

Let us take a brief look at the most important political ideologies dating back to *Aristotle*.[8] In *monarchies* there is one ruler and the distribution of values is made according to status, in *oligarchies* the distribution is made according to one's due, and in *democracies* the distribution is in principle equal.

But to Aristotle the three political ideal types had a positive and a negative variant as well. Monarchy matches with tyranny, oligarchy with aristocracy, and democracy with »vulgar democracy«. Vulgar democracy is unprincipled, whereas genuine democracy reflects the »reasonable common will« of the people according to general rules. Democracy must thus have an inherent *morality* and first of all respect the principle of *justice*, which has two facets: The *commutative* and *distributive* justice.[9] The first and oldest, pre-state variant demands *equality* of performance and payment, wrong and retribution (an eye for an eye), and the second one demands reward according to one's *utility* in society. In both cases remuneration must respect the »*due*« of the individual and »equal treatment of equal cases«. Aristotle's ideology was not equality in general, but equality within each group of people.

It was the later *stoic philosophy* which claimed the equality of all human beings, as they were part of the divine creation and therefore also part of divine reason. The stoic principle of equality in imperial Rome was mixed with Christian equality justified almost in the same way. The political practice now and especially later in the mediaeval feudal society was, however, different. The *Augustinian* philosophy of the Divine State and the two swords was built upon the hierarchial system of the feudal society, with the secular princes subordinated the Church, whose interests they were to protect in return for the divine justification of their power.

It is also perfectly clear that a poor agrarian society has not the sufficient surplus to treat each individual equally. The principle of equality and democracy presupposes a certain amount of wealth and division of labour, which do not exist until the great discoveries in the 15th century. Already the 13th century Renaissance had revived the idea of human power of legislation together with the individualistic conception of man based on reason. But a radical, individualistic political and legal ideology was not formulated until the teachings of *Grotius* and *Hobbes* in different versions in the middle of the 17th century revived the idea of social contract, which in the 18th century developed into a revolutionary theory of human rights and democracy.

The original *idea* of democracy of that time was, like Aristotle's philosophy, based upon the presupposition of a *reasonable debate among enlightened people*. The *reality* of democracy was rather, as realized one century later by *Rudolph von Jhering* and *Karl Marx*, a struggle about the law, which became the meeting point of conflicting *social interests*.[10] Jhering believed in the freedom of the individual and the state, whereas Marx found that the interests of society were most important. In that respect socialism concurs with conservatism by emphasizing the collectivistic interests of the totality and the individuals as parts of that, and both are in principle antagonistic to liberalism, which regards society as an association of *individuals*. Already in the middle of the 19th century *John Stuart Mill* tried to mediate the original thinking of Jeremy Bentham and Adam Smith. *Bentham* argued that »social utility« was the leading value in law and morals, and *Smith* that the egoistic actions of the individuals by means of a »hidden hand« would tend to create the optimal utility for society. Later research has proved that Smith's »hidden hand« was remnants of the Continental natural law theory and its assumption that man is not only a rational but also a social being (zoon politikon).[11] Stuart Mill did not believe that the egoistic endeavours of the human nature automatically leads to the benefit of society and, like Jhering, called for the intervention of legislation in order to obtain social utility.

In the beginning of this century the utilitarian and the socialist ideology concurred with the naturalistic conception of man and logical empiricism, which together formed the presupposed basis of the rebuilding of the Western democracies after World War II. Economic growth became the aim and not the means of politics, and social utility was not questioned as the leading value, the *distribution* of goods becoming the major issue of democratic policy.

When prosperity became self-evident for a new generation, an ideological explosion occured in the 1960s with a frontal attack on logical positivism, which was regarded as the theoretical justification of the reduction of morality and politics to concern social utility and the distribution of wealth, »rationality« and »efficiency« becoming the criteria of the right action. All parties, leftists, rightists and liberals, opposed the »technological society« and the »one-dimensional man«.

The *Marxists* recommended an »alternative« society, in which the individuals would fit in without any »contradiction«, if only the private property right to the means of production be abolished. Liberty and equality would automatically occur when the contradiction between public utility and individual freedom thus vanished. *Liberals* from the other corner criticized the deprival of capacity and

62

individual responsibility which resulted from the conception of individuals as victims of internal and external forces.

The Norwegian criminologist *Nils Christie* provocatively attacked the indeterminate sentence of criminals, naming it »theft of responsibility«, with Solsjenitsyn's description of the Gulag as a horrifying accompaniment.[12] The American moral philosopher *John Rawls*[13] returned to the classical theory of social contract, claiming that the interests of society have a high priority but cannot entirely outbalance the interests of the individual. The *social utility* must therefore compete with *individual justice* in the last resort.

Rawls tries to balance *freedom* and *equality*, assuming that all rational people would prefer an equal distribution of values, if their »strategic position« was hidden behind a »veil of ignorance«. From that hypothetical starting point of a social contract he derives a form of a social-democratic society with equality as the basic value, which must give way only when concessions to liberty creating an unequal distribution lead to a situation, where the »poorest« people are »better off«. It is not easy to say who the »poorest« are and what »better off« is, and it is definitely an unrealistic assumption that all people are »rational«. But as a model of *the process* of creating a just society - *justice as fairness* - it is an attempt to mitigate distributive justice with commutative justice which demands a proportionality between performance and payment.

The subsequent discussion of Rawls' ideas shows that later years of economic stagnation seems to call for a stimulation of productivity at the expense of equality and distributive justice. On the other hand tolerance seems to decrease in times of recession. In the 70s we realized how Western societies under the pressure of the oil crisis and stagflation tried to »distribute« poverty by taxation and forget about the *effectiveness* of public utility on the one hand and individual justice on the other.

The best may become an enemy of the good. As *Alex de Tocqueville* profetically put it 150 years ago: The smaller inequalities become in society, the less bearable be the remaining ones. Maybe the American economist *Kenneth Arrow*[14] was right, when he matematically proved that a rational distribution of values is a logical impossibility under a democratic rule, and mediates *effectiveness* and social utility with equality and *individual justice*.

Notes

1) *B. F. Skinner*, Beyond Freedom and Dignity (1971).
2) *Stig Jørgensen*, Values in Law: Ideas, Principles and Rules (1978) p. 9 ff.
3) *Stig Jørgensen*, Pluralis Juris (1982) p. 7 ff.; *same*, Recht und Gesellschaft (1970) p. 38 ff.; *same*, Vertrag und Recht (1968).

4) *Stig Jørgensen*, Values in Law (l.c. note 2) p. 151 ff.; *same*, Typologie und »Realismus« in der neueren Rechtswissenschaft (1971); *same*, On Meaning, Opinion and Argumentation, in: Reasoning on Legal Reasoning, ed. by A. Peczenik and J. Uusitalo (1979) p. 87 ff.

5) *Stig Jørgensen*, Values in Law (l.c. note 2) p. 9 ff.

6) *Stig Jørgensen*, Pluralis Juris (l.c. note 3)

7) See *Stig Jørgensen*, Values in Law (l.c. note 2) p. 59; *same*, Demokratie und Völkerbewegung, in: Filosofía del Derecho y Filosofía Politica, Memoria del X Congresso Mundial Ordinario de Filosofía del Derecho y Filosofía Social, Vol. II, Mexico 1981, p. 83 ff.

8) *Stig Jørgensen*, The Crisis of Democracy, below p. 150

9) *Stig Jørgensen*, Values in Law (l.c. note 2) p. 59 ff.; *same*, Ethik und Gerechtigkeit (1980) p. 23 ff.

10) *Stig Jørgensen*, Die Bedeutung Jherings für die neuere skandinavische Rechtswissenschaft, in: Jherings Erbe, hrsg. von F. Wieacker und Chr. Wollschläger (1970) p. 118.

11) *Peter Stein*, Adam Smith's Jurisprudence, in: Cornell Law Review (1979) p. 621 ff.

12) *Nils Christie*, Limits to Pain (1981).

13) *John Rawls*, A Theory of Justice (1971); see *Stig Jørgensen*, Values in Law (l.c. note 2) p. 151 ff., and *same*, Pluralis Juris (l.c. note 3) p. 24 ff.

14) *Kenneth Arrow*, Social Choice and Individual Values (Yale 1951).

What is Law?

The point of my book *Pluralis Juris*[1] is to stress the fact that truth, like God, has many faces. The same goes with law, which must be defined according to the different relations in which it is involved. This means, of course, that the definition is dependent on the specific function law performs in a certain relation. It does not mean that it is irrelevant which meaning of law we choose; relationism does not mean the same as relativism.

For lawyers in general, law in the *dogmatic sense* is decisive. For the actual lawyer living in the modern state, the problem of valid law is the essential one. For the legal scientist this aspect of law is also essential, but less simple. In principle, the criterion is what creates a legal obligation. However, this involves complicated questions of identifying the sources of law and of separating law from reality and from other social obligations. The interpretation of the sources of law is itself a complex matter which implies teleological as well as pragmatic considerations. This is connected with the application of law in concrete cases, actual as well as hypothetical. One must remember that law is not an independent semiotic system or an autonomous literal or illiteral system of signs like a literary text, a poem, etc., but a normative system, the purpose of which is to affect human behaviour; therefore, interpretation cannot be separated from application.

But law cannot only be studied as an axiomatic system of obligations and duties. It is possible to study it more *comparatively*,[2] i.e. as a phenomenon, from an external point of view: what is law? and not, as in the dogmatic sense, from an internal point of view: what is valid law according to the actual Danish/English/Australian legal system? You can make vertical as well as horizontal comparisons. By vertical comparisons I understand legal-historical points of view, and by horizontal comparisons I understand comparisons between the actual legal system in one country and the legal systems in other countries.

It goes without saying that both kinds of comparisons do not make sense without taking the function of law and legal institutions into account; it is necessary to take a functional or factual approach. This brings us to an other kind of horizontal comparison: the comparison of the legal rules and the social system, which is the viewpoint of the sociology of law. We can study law not only from a strictly empirical point of view and put a question of the type: how is law? and from a hermeneutical point of view by putting questions of the kind: why is law as it is? but we can also raise critical or legal-political questions of the type: why is law not different? That means that law must also be analysed as part of political ideologies, not only according to the purposes of an actual working political system but also as a means of changing the organisation of society.

Of course, this *political* and ideological approach to the study and analysis of law is important, but it is also problematic. Political approaches to law often tend to be paranoiac. In my view this has been the case especially with the Marxist analysis of law as a means of suppression.[3] At Karl Marx's time, in the second half of the 19th century, it was a fruitful new perspective to see law as an expression not of ideas but of concrete human interests. It was not the invention of Karl Marx but the common basis of the historicism which prevailed in Europe at that time.[4] Evolution had become the central concern of the sciences at the beginning of the century, when natural philosophy - as the Danish physicist and discoverer of electromagnetism, H. C. Ørsted, put it - sought the spirit in nature. As dialectics was the paradigm of the medieval sciences (including legal science), and as mathematics and astronomy were the models of the sciences of the Renaissance and the time of the Enlightenment, so biology and electricty became the models of the 19th century sciences. Goethe and Herder had already pointed at the organic nature of culture, and Jeremy Bentham had stressed its dynamism identifying the creation of happiness as its purpose. In Germany, F. C. von Savigny had emphasized the historical foundation of law, finding its source in the spirit of the people and claiming that it evolved in the same, organic way as language and culture. In doing so, Savigny was, of course, acting politically, because he used this approach to reject the proposition of his colleague. A. F. J. Thibaut, to create a general German codification akin to French Napoleonic law. Both Thibaut and Savigny were pupils of the German philosopher Immanuel Kant, who was himself inspired by the French Revolution and the idea of human liberty. Liberty presupposed human society, as responsibility is illogical if there is no human freedom of action. Immanuel Kant also presupposed the necessity of natural laws which governed empirical reality as a condition for cognition. The French Revolution, however, did not create the liberal state based on human freedom which Kant foresaw - but the Napoleonic empire, dominated by the will of the sovereign or the State.

That was exactly what Savigny meant when he argued against Thibaut. In the first place he did not want French law in Germany, in the second place he did not want the State to interfere with the private sphere. Therefore, Savigny not only developed the concept of a science of law as opposed to jurisprudence, but also introduced a separation between public law and private law. Public law was to deal with the limited objects of »the nightwatch state« to preserve peace externally and internally. The State should keep out of its private relations of its citizens, which were to be left entirely to the ordering of the private will.

Savigny initially adopted a sociological approach by starting his legal analyses with the »conditions of life« *(Lebensverhältnisse)* and the »conditions of law« *(Rechtsverhältnisse)*, which grew out of the former. On the other hand, he regarded legal institutions as the static elements of the dynamic history of law, which led him to the absurd position of regarding Roman law as the source of the German law. In order to protect German law from new influence by foreign law and from being dominated by the state, his originally sociological approach to law turned into a speculative system of concepts derived from the general idea of liberty as developed in an ancient and foreign Roman society. Of course, this shift could be formally justified by the fact that Roman law had been received in the Middle Ages by the German emperors as subsidiary law for the whole empire, as a sort of common law in case the positive law of the different states in the empire could not supply an answer to a legal question.

Although the law which emerged from the efforts of the »Romanists« between the 12th century and the 19th century was completely different from the original classical and even from the revised Justinian Roman law, the »Pandects« of Savigny and his successors, Puchta and Windscheid, were still very much detached from the social needs in Germany in and during the first half of the 19th century.

Not only the Germanist school of law criticized the conceptual and unrealistic legal science. The most important critique of the conceptual school of legal science was written by one of its most brilliant former members, Rudolph von Jhering, who distanced himself from it in a series of publications.[5] Inspired by Jeremy Bentham and John Stuart Mill, on the one hand, and the philosophy of Schopenhauer on the other, he saw the law as the outcome of a political struggle *(Kampf ums Recht)* between different social interests. In his analysis subjective rights were legally protected interests, and objective law was the instrument by which the forces dominating the political system could control and change conditions in society in accordance with their own purposes. Like the social democrat Lassalle, and unlike Karl Marx, Jhering believed in the capacity of law to influence social processes and to change the legal positions of individuals and groups in society.

Here we stand at the crucial point of the dichotomy of law and society. Karl Marx believed that law belonged to the superstructure and not to the material basis of society which determines the structure and power in society. Law, like religion, literature and so on, belonged to the ideology of the society, which, according to Marx, necessarily is a false consciousness as long as the means of production are privately owned, because such societies are founded on a contradiction between the owners and the workers, who are robbed of the surplus value of their labour by the proprietors, who thereby suppress the working class. So that these facts might be hidden from the worker, his mind is distorted by means of religion, law and culture, which depict the suppression of the workers as a natural order of things.

According to this Marxist conception of law, society cannot be changed by legal means, but only by means of a revolution, which becomes a historical necessity for dialectical materialism. In states where a so-called Marxist revolution has been carried through, the party in power accepts and uses this conception of law in order to justify the dictatorship of the proletariat and the suppression of the bourgeois elements of the old society. At the same time they accept another definition of law which contrasts sharply with the original Marxian conception of law as a mere reflection of material conditions. All Socialist countries have adopted the Kelsenian definition of law as the command of the state backed by the threats of organized power, and the identification of state and law as two different expressions of the same reality.

Of course, Rudolph von Jhering did not mean that law was independent of social conditions. On the contrary, he stressed that law was the result of social processes and political struggle. As he once put it: eine Handlung ohne Motiv ist wie eine Wirkung ohne Ursache (an act without a motive is like an effect without a cause) and: just as you cannot make an engine move by talking to it about the laws of motion, you cannot make a human being act by confronting him with the categoric imperative.

Jhering's naturalistic conception of law led to two different movements in German legal theory: the so-called *Freirechtsschule* and the so-called *Interessenjurisprudenz*. The former, which is related to the so-called American sociological jurisprudence, leaves it to the judge to make his decision according to all circumstances involved in a concrete case, whereas the latter stresses the teleological nature of law, which requires the judge to seek his inspiration in the actual or supposed purpose of the law. During recent years this theory has developed into a so-called *Wertungsjurisprudenz*, which stresses the fact that the politico-legal system must be regarded as an emanation of an underlying system of values which expresses the general culture of the country, although it may be shared to a smaller or greater extent by other countries which have inherited the same cultural traditions.

Law can also be interpreted as a *cultural phenomenon* consisting of those rules which make human cooperation in society possible.[6] Of course, law in this sense is partly a natural phenomenon built into human nature as instincts and emotions, as it is the case with other animals who live in groups. This must be the case if the human race is to survive, since its reproduction depends on the bringing up of babies who are helpless for a number of years and dependent on a family which can nurse them and supply them and their mothers with the necessary food and protection.

The relation between the size of a baby's head and the mother's anatomy dictates a premature birth, and requires the former to develop its full physical and spiritual abilities outside the womb. This has permitted the human race, alone among the animal species, to expand its brain capacity to a point where it has become capable of abstract thinking and reflection. This faculty, which is closely connected with language, enables man to shape ideas and concepts which symbolically represent reality. The concept and the feeling of rights and duties, for example, represents one particular perception of social reality. On the other hand, the human species is deficient in instincts compared with other animal species. This gives man a high degree of freedom for creating and changing his environment and for adapting the outer world to his needs and desires and so to create culture, although it is also possible to regard the ideas, the institutions and the rules, which are created as part of the culture, as the substitutes for the instincts which govern the societies of the animals.

It is, of course, not possible to separate law from *morality and even religion*[7] in these original societies, and it is perhaps not meaningful at all to speak about law in this context. Yet, it would be a mistake to define law out of existence in societies, which do not have the formal legal institutions known in modern, developed societies. As mentioned before, in modern societies there also exists a close connection between law and general culture, represented by the values which are the general background of the legal-political system.

However, a major part of a modern legal system is of a technical nature and is as such not covered by the moral system. Moreover, other parts of the positive law may be contrary to moral precepts. Some natural law or ethical theories regard such rules as invalid, especially when the positive law infringes major principles, e.g. basic human rights. Other legal theories take a positivistic or analytical stand and regard such rules as valid when they are actually effective and upheld in society. As a representative of such modern positivistic, analytical theory, Herbert Hart stresses the need for clarity in analyses, and instead of talking of invalid law he talks about immoral law.

Furthermore, Herbert Hart isolates what he calls the minimum content of law by extracting the common core of all historical legal systems. He does not regard this minimum content as a condition of the validity of a legal system, but rather as a condition of the functioning of a society. Peace, order and predictability are preconditions for the functioning of any social group. Therefore, there must be rules against murder, assault, theft and fraud. There must also be some protection of the family and the authority of society. We may point at the Ten Commandments as a representation of principles which comprise the minimum content of law in a primitive society: you must not kill, you must not steal, you must not lie, but tell the truth so that you can be depended upon. The first and the second Commandments refer to cultural and social conditions where respect may be regarded as relative. That does not mean that the other commandments contain no relative elements which can be modified in the course of history, but it means that the two first Commandments reflect two essential elements in pre-state law.

The first of these is the Commandment that you shall fear your God. I think that it is fair to say that all the high cultures of the world identify a religious source of their law. Moses went to the top of Mount Sinai and came down with the tables of the law conveyed to him by God. It is not possible to give a precise dating of Mosaic law, but the Old Testament was written through a period of about 600 years from 1000 B.C. until 400 B.C., the Pentateuch belonging to the older part of the texts. Even older is Hammurabi's law given by the Semitic ruler of Babylon about 1600 B.C. In the preamble to this law Hammurabi presents himself as the mediator between the gods and people; the laws have been handed down to Hammurabi by the gods, so that he, in turn, can demand obedience from the people. From paintings in pharaonic graves we know that the Egyptians also believed that the laws were of divine origin; and there is no doubt about the religious source of law in the later Greek and Roman societies.

At the same time, it is true that the Greeks were the first to develop a positivistic conception of law. The Sophists in the 5th century argued that, just as gods did not create man, but man created the gods, so law was not created by the gods but by man by means of a social contract which is reflected in the political democracy of Athens. Another interesting feature in this picture is that the Athenians, because of their political system, never created a legal science or legal profession, because legal disputes were settled at the people's assembly in the same way as statutes were inacted by voting of the assembled citizens. There was no need for legal argumentation but for rhetorical argumentation, the art of which reached a peak in that period.

By the same token, this extreme democracy, after the execution of Socrates and the disasters of the Peloponnesian war, gave rise to the criticism of Plato and

Aristotle, both of whom condemned the immorality of the vulgar democracy, as Aristotle named it, and both of whom advocated instead that politico-legal decisions should be based on principles.[8] But while Plato proposed a sort of communistic dictatorship of the philosophers, Aristotle advocated a principled democracy where the reasonable will of all citizens should not be confused with the actual will of a crowd seduced by flatterers.

The emergence of democracy in Greece is perhaps bound up with the geographical conditions of the country which permitted only the forming of small communities which could communicate only by sea - which in turn encouraged commerce and the exchange of goods. It is reasonable to claim that democracy presupposes a certain amount of wealth, which can only be produced by a division of labour, and after the idea of money has become accepted. These developments encouraged the notion of an individual who has his own rights and duties according to his deserts.

The history of Rome was different. After the old Tarquin kings had been deposed, an aristocratic republic took over, governed by the patricians, the plebeians being without civil rights. Gradually, this situation became intolerable for the plebeians who eventually made a compromise with the patricians who gave them a share of the political power vested in new officers, the tribunes. They operated alongside the original consuls and praetor, who admistered and developed the old Roman formular system. It was a so-called process-type system, which, like the later medieval English system, meant that a legal right was dependent on the availability of a remedy and not the other way round. The Roman concept of *actio* and the English *writ* are relics of the old conflict solution which was originally a completely private affair.[9] Nevertheless, it was the Romans and not the Greeks who invented a legal science and a legal profession.

In the old prestate societies[10] the family or the tribe is the social unit which takes care of the individual, who in turn has a right to his share of the outcome of the joint venture of the group or family. Thus, old people in these old static societies are held in high esteem, for they represent what is most highly valued: experience. And although they can no longer participate in the direct productive process they are provided with sufficient resources to survive. The children, on their side, represent the future maintenance of the parents, even if they are not yet able to render much actual assistance. When conflicts occur between groups there are no rules and no mechanisms to solve the problem peacefully. The only reaction against violation of one group by another is revenge, and in most primitive cultures the family or kin takes care of retribution against the other group, because not the individual but the collective is the smallest unit of society.

In the long run a society which has developed its economic system cannot tolerate such an unlimited chain of revenge. In order to keep peace, revenge is first restricted to the so-called talion, i.e. revenge must not go further than the violation. An expression of this is found in Mosaic law, which states that you must take an eye for an eye and a tooth for a tooth and life for a life. Mosaic law also contains a further development, in that the revenge or talion can be commuted into a sum of money, a fine. This transformation seems to occur at a certain stage of the evolution of all societies. Already in Hammurabi's law, in the Draconian law of Athens around 600 B.C., and in the Twelve Tables of Rome from about 450 B.C. we find a more or less developed system of commutation. Later on, in medieval Europe we find the same development. In the Scandinavian »landscape« laws from the 12th and 13th centuries the transformation has only just taken place, which is indicated by some presuppositions which still reflect the old law.

The socio-economic situation in which the transformation takes place is supposed to be an agrarian society which, because of the long period of time between the sowing and the harvesting of the crops, is very vulnerable and requires internal peace. A general feature of these systems is that the fines are assessed according to certain classified weights, regardless of the individual circumstances. The only exclusion is that very important people can demand »overfines«, and that some violations cannot be commuted into a fine. It is a general theory that these rates were elaborated through the practice of mediators who literally went between the parties and worked out a compromise. Later on, mediators were replaced by arbitrators who were elected by the parties with the power of making decisions which were binding for them. Evidence in support of the first assertion can be found in ancient Greek history. In the *Iliad* there is a scene where the goddess, Dike, throws her stick between the conflicting parties - the symbolic meaning of the sceptre of the goddess of justice represents the physical fact of going between the parties by throwing a stick. The second assertion can be supported by the fact that the Roman *judex*, judge, was not appointed by the authorities until imperial times, but was an arbitrator who was elected by the parties.

The next step in the development of social and legal ideas happened in the Mediterranean area around 450 B.C. Until then legal ideology was collectivistic, objective and casuistic. After that time, not only in Athens and Rome, but also in Palestine, legal and social ideology became individualistic, subjective and generalising. In the New Testament it is the individual who is responsible for his acts and who is bound by his contracts. It is not the family who is responsible, and the individual is not responsible for his father's sins. On the other hand, he is only responsible when his action has been a wilful act, and ideology is expressed in general rules like the fundamental rule, that we should love our neighbour. In

Greece the same development is illustrated in the contrast between the *Oresteia* of Aischylos, in which the harsh tribal society of revenge is still dominant, and Sophocles' *Antigone*, written a generation later, in which a higher natural law permits the individual to violate old tribal customs. Rome, at the time of the Twelve Tables, also shows a transition to an individualistic conception of man and his rights. The individual was seen as deserving not more and not less than the equivalent of what he has performed. As a consequence, old people and children were becoming worthless. In order to protect them, a change in general morality had to occur, and it took the form of the Christian commitment to mercy. The Old Testament Commandment, to honour one's father and mother, had no longer a place in this changed social environment. Instead, the individual was expected to honour the authority of the state and the law.

The revelation of law by the gods points to another important feature of law: its publicity. It is not an accident that the laws of Moses were written on stone, that Hammurabi's laws were also carved in stone, and that the Draconian penal laws and the Twelve Tables in Rome were all exhibited in the city square.

It is beyond any doubt that this is all part of the development of civilisation. Here, I do not want to go into the many theories about why cultures broke down, but I simply point to the fact that the refined legal system and legal science fell with them, and that Europe in the Middle Ages, as far as law is concerned, had to make a fresh start in a fragmented and subsistence-oriented, feudal society which had forgotten the *pax Romana* and lacked any organisation which could have secured peace outside the small units dominated by feudal princes. This meant that legal thinking returned to a primitive stage of collectivity, objectivity and casuistry.

It was not until the Renaissance that the economy began to produce again a significant surplus, first in the North Italian merchant cities, and later in the whole of Western Europe, after the great discoveries at the end of the 15th century. The ideal of the Renaissance was classical Greek and Roman culture, and there is a tradition that in the second half of the 11th century a copy of the *Corpus Juris* was found in Bologna just as the philosophical writings of Aristotle were handed over to the Europeans by the Arabs who had preserved them. Now legal science could again begin to come into its own. First, the legal texts were annotated between the lines and in the margin without any reflection on their applicability in practical life; later, the commentators studied Roman law against the background of their own social and political situation. They used the resulting conglomerate as material in the administration of the growing bureaucracies of the princes who needed professional assistance during the later medieval years. As mentioned earlier, the German emperors introduced into their realm the modified Roman law created by this Romanistic science as a kind of common law, partly because there was a desperate need for a new and developed legal materials, partly because they wished to signal that they were the legal heirs of the ancient Roman emperors.

As long as the upholding of the legal system was left to the individual families and the tribes, conflicts were solved not on the basis of evidence but on the basis of oaths which were not concerned with facts but with the credibility of the parties. Although the theory of legal responsibility was elaborated by medieval canon law, this did not affect secular law until much later; and it was not until the second half of the 18th century that negligence came to be regarded as a general precondition for civil liability. Catholic moral theology also played a role in the development of the modern conception of law.[11] It developed a theory of *justum pretium*, based on the ancient Greek idea of justice as a proportionate justice, which taught that there should be a fair relation between the value of the performance of one party and what he got in return. It also taught that promises of the individual should be binding in principle, which was not always the case in secular law, as in Roman law only certain types of contracts were legally binding.

Through Hugo Grotius' writings this moral philosophy influenced the so-called natural law which created an ideology of the *individual's rights*[12] and of the concept of the binding contract, not only as a foundation of private law but also as a foundation of the state as a social contract. This rationalistic natural law, which was developed from the beginning of the 17th to the end of the 18th century through a combination of Roman law, Greek philosophy and Christian moral philosophy created the material for the later great codifications of Western Europe and modern legal science.

It is important to appreciate at this point that Russia, in the creative years from the middle of the 13th to the middle of the 15th century, was occupied by the Tartars who exploited and suppressed the population. That kept the Russians outside the sphere influenced by the Renaissance and its creation of an *individualistic ideology* and, on the legal side, the idea that the human being has formal, legal rights, irrespective of his political, religious and moral beliefs. This may have been why Russia never became part of Western civilization and never accepted the concept of a formal human right and a democratic, political ideology. According to that interpretation the totalitarian Soviet system is not a product of Marxist-Leninism, but a reflection of traditional Russian administrative thinking. The Russian czars and czarinas tried, or pretended to try, to import Western civilization and Western law into Russia, but the social conditions were unsuitable, and when Peter the Great at the beginning of the 18th century tried to import European military and commercial law, he succeeded only with military law.

The great reforms of the Russian legal system in the direction of the rule of law in the second half of the 19th and the beginning of the 20th century were stopped, first by several uprisings and at last by the revolution in 1917. Nevertheless, it is crucial to understand, in the context of a general theory of *reception of law*,[13] that commercial law in the modern sense simply could not work in czarist society, where there was little or no commerce at all. Moreover, commerce cannot function if society has not accepted a concept of formal legal rules, which apply, irrespective of religious, ideological and moral censorship, as commerce can function only if the behaviour of the participants can be predicted over time.

This is the reason why developing countries need to import large parts of a developed legal system - in particular, its private law aspects. Japan, for example, when it was opened to European influence in the last years of the 19th century, formally received the German civil code, and Turkey adopted the Swiss civil code after the First World War. India and many other English colonies received the English common law in order to cope with their need to regulate and encourage production and trade. Yet, law transplanted to a foreign culture has a general tendency to work only insofar as is necessary to deal with practical problems; other parts are rarely applied or blend with the old customary laws, so that the result, after some time, differs quite significantly from the imported model.

In addition, law is not, even in modern times, limited to the official state legislation. In Scandinavia, for instance, may *other sources of law* still operate, especially in the tort law which is still largely elaborated in *customary law*. *Court practice* is also a source of law, together with academic *legal writing*, to which not only Danish courts often refer, to justify the view on certain points of law adopted by them. To these sources others, like international conventions and standard commercial practices, must be added. There is no doubt that materials of the latter kind have legal force if the parties have agreed to their application, but they can also bind the parties, if this is not the case - for example, if they belong to a professional group which usually follows a certain practice.

I have tried to show in this paper[14] that the development of law and legal science goes hand in hand with the general development of culture and civilization, and that law is, on the one hand, dependent on these extra-legal factors and, on the other hand, a major means of shaping civilization and culture. There is no need to restrict the general concept of law to what is regarded as modern, developed, state system; law has at all times had the function of keeping the peace and of permitting society to operate under the conditions prevailing at that time. Therefore, norms and rules, which cannot be state law, since they apply in stateless societies, or to the relations between states, must be seen as falling within this broad concept of law. This also applies to the private production of legal materials in modern state-societies. Parliaments simply do not have the ability to produce all the legal materials required, nor do they have the necessary professional skills in certain fields.

I have placed particular stress on the Western European invention of an *individualistic concept of personal and human rights*, since this was a pre-condition for the development of modern industrial technology and for the creation of formal legal rules which can cope with the complicated matter and create a predictability of behaviour which is necessary for sustained economic growth. I have also stressed a negative consequence of this development. The underlying individualistic ideology has created a crisis for modern Western democracy which can no longer harmonize the economic need for increased capital investments with the political desire to distribute as much of the economic surplus as possible among the current population. The Japanese and other Asian cultures, which have not created the scientific or the legal conditions for the mass production, because of their ways of collective thinking and collective social organisation, do not have the same difficulty in controlling modern industry; there is no conflict between the factories and the workers, both of whom are perceived as parts of the same collective.

The fundamental argument behind this analysis of law is simply that law has *different functions* and that *legal science* must consequently have *different departments*.

The *political functions* of law can best be studied by political and economic science, while *social* and *psychological* functions should be studied by sociology and social psychology, and its *cultural* functions by ethnology. *History* of law and *comparative* legal science compare legal rules and their social functions in a vertical, or horizontal perspective. It is common to all these parts of legal science that they do not aim at describing and interpreting valid or current law. Therefore, their methods will in principle be descriptive, i.e. they describe the law as part of working political, social, psychological and cultural systems.

Against this stands *dogmatic legal science* which is the original and practically the most important part of legal science. The task of this science is the interpretation of the authoritative rule material, the valid or current law. Dogmatic legal science describes law systematically and by means of a number of authoritative sources of law and a number of methods of argumentation coined throughout history, which are accepted by jurists and correspond to the method of argumentation applied in legal practice. Some of these features refer to normative elements (justice, fairness, equity), others to linguistic, logical elements and yet others to elements of reality (teleological and pragmatic considerations).

When legal philosophers have attempted to devise a general concept of law, they have often used a dogmatic legal science as their only point of reference. On the other hand, attempts to disregard dogmatic law and to treat legal science as a social science have also been unsuccessful, because they have been of little interest to the main customer: the legal profession. For the same reason a strictly analytical (pure) theory of law has been no great success either. The debate between legal science and legal philosophy will probably go on until legal philosophy realizes and respects the fact that law has different aspects according to its different functions, and that legal science must therefore apply different methods.

The content of the concept of law in a given situation must depend on the *kind of question* asked, which in turn depends on the specific roles or functions performed by the legal actor involved. The consulting lawyer is most interested in the probability of a certain decision in a prospective law suit, whereas the judge is in no need of such an external definition but must ascertain the rules he is obliged to apply. Like the judges, dogmatic legal science is interested in the internal aspect of law, not only in connection with the solution of actual problems, but in order to be able to present the individual solutions or rules as parts of a systematic, consistent whole. Legal sociology and social psychology are interested in current law, i.e. rules of behaviour which are actually complied with or which are felt to be obligatory. The main interest of the politicians is in the regulating effect, or the coercive character, of the law. In this respect, special importance must be given to the question of power and sanctions, although models of democratic government rely to a large extent on the public acceptance of the legal system and its individual rules. History of law, ethnology and international law take, for different reasons, less interest in the aspect of enforcement, but want to see law as part of the national and international patterns of culture. The church and the ideological movements in the widest sense conceive law as a realization of a superior order: the course of nature, the nature of man, the will of God, reason or justice (natural law). They are therefore unable to respect positive law unconditionally, because to them its content may be invalid, in which case they have a right and a duty to resist it (right of resistance, civil disobedience).

If a *programmatic* or *ideological* definition of law is chosen, it must reflect an underlying general conception of man and society. A command theory corresponds with an authoritarian state concept and collective concept of man. A sociological, functional theory of law may be the expression of a collective concept of man, too, since social utility and distributive justice are regarded as the supreme values. A theory based on the individual rights of man looks upon man as an individual and nothing else, and assigns to society the minimal task of securing these individual rights. A pluralistic legal philosophy, which regards man as an individual, and as a social being, must recognize that social utility and individual justice are competing values of equal importance, so the latter cannot be seen as forming merely a minor part of distributive justice. A manifestation of this fact is an increasing tendency within legal philosophy during the last decade to focus again on those aspects of law which are concerned with the individual, at the expense of its regulative as well as its distributive functions, which claimed attention during the previous half-century.

Notes

1) S. Jørgensen, *Pluralis Juris* (Aarhus, 1982), see also *idem, Law and Society* (Copenhagen, 1971).
2) *Idem, Vertrag und Recht*, Copenhagen, 1968, pp. 111 ff.
3) *Idem, Values in Law*, 1978, pp. 9 ff.
4) *Idem, Vertrag und Recht, supra n.* 2, at 49 ff., especially 64 ff.; *Law and Society, supra n.* 1, at 60 ff.
5) *Idem,* »Die Bedeutung Jherings für die neuere skandinavische Rechtslehre. Jherings Erbe«, Göttinger Symposium zur 150. Wiederkehr des Geburtstags von Rudolph von Jhering, F. Wieacker and C. Wollschläger (eds), Göttingen, 1970, p. 116. See also *Values in Law, supra n.* 3, at 121.
6) *Idem, Law and Society, supra n.* 1, at 4 and 31. See also *idem, Pluralis Juris, supra n.* 1; »The Contract«, unpublished; »Private Property. Regulation and Governmental Direction«, in W. Krawietz, T. Mayer-Maly, O. Weinberger (eds), *Objektivierung des Rechtsdenkens*, Berlin, 1984, p. 615.
7) *Idem,* »The Contract«, *supra n.* 6; *Values in Law, supra n.* 3, at 59 ff. and 103; *Law and Society, supra n.* 1 at 27; »*Gut* und *böse* in Wandel des Rechtsauffassungen«, in *Ethik und Gerechtigkeit*, Göttingen, 1980, p. 7. See also H. Berman *The Interaction of Law and Religion* (London, 1974).
8) S. Jørgensen, »Demokratie und Völkerbewegung«, in *Filosofía del Derecho y Filisofía Politica*, Memoria del X Congreso Mundial Ordinario de Filosofía del Derecho y Filosofía Social, Mexico, 1981, vol. 2, 83 ff.
9) K. H. Ziegler, Das private Schiedsgericht im antiken römischen Recht; M. Steinberg, »The Twelve Tables and their Origins«, (1982) 42 *Journal of the History of Ideas*, 379 ff.
10) S. Jørgensen, *Ethik und Gerechtigkeit, supra n.* 7, at 12 ff.; *Law and Society, supra n.* 1, at 69; *Values in Law, supra n.* 3, at 65.
11) *Idem, Vertrag und Recht, supra n.* 2, at 141; »Die skandinavische Lehre der Vertragsverletzung«, Festschrift für Karl Larenz, 1973, pp. 59 ff.; *Law and Society, supra n.* 1, at 65 ff.; *Values in Law, supra n.* 2, at 59 ff.

12) *Idem*, »Private Property«, *supra n.* 6; »The Contract«, *supra n.* 6.

13) *Idem, Vertrag und Recht, supra n.* 2, at 119; *Law and Society, supra n.* 1, at 59. See also F. Wieacker, *Privatrechtsgeschichte der Neuzeit*, 2 ed., Göttingen, 1967, p. 124; »Zum heutigen Stand der Rezeptionsforschung«, Festschrift für Joseph Klein, 1967, p. 196; J. Zajtay, Zum Begriff der Gesamtrezeption fremder Rechte (1970) *Archiv für die zivilistische Praxis*, 251; M. Rehbinder, »Die Rezeption fremden Rechts in soziologischer Sicht« (1983) 14 *Rechtstheorie*, 305.

14) *Idem, Pluralis Juris, supra n.* 1.

Scandinavian Legal Philosophy

By »Scandinavian legal philosophy« is nowadays meant - almost without exception - the variant of a »realistic legal theory« called »Scandinavian realism«. Scandinavian realism has its philosophical foundation in the theoretical and practical philosophy of the Swede Axel Hägerström from the beginning of this century. Its most outstanding representatives are said to be the Swedes Vilhelm Lundstedt and Karl Olivecrona and the Dane Alf Ross.[1]

Like practically all other truths this one is also a qualified truth. In the first place the realistic tradition within Nordic legal philosophy, »Nordic realism«, dates much further back, secondly »Scandinavian realism« had a limited influence on the legal sciences of the other Nordic countries, thirdly it is for several reasons inaccurate to include Alf Ross among the representatives of »Scandinavian realism«.[2]

Legal Realism

Legal Realism can mean different things. First of all, it is by this term usually meant the opposite of *Natural Law*, which usually implies one of two things: that the *source* of law is found in transcendent phenomena: the will of God, the natural order, human reason, the idea of justice, or that its *content* must be subject to control by justice which means that it must be in accordance with some general moral principles like human rights and the rule of law. In opposition to a natural law conception legal realism finds its sources in immanent phenomena: custom, the will of a sovereign, or legislation. In this respect legal realism is identical with legal positivism, and Scandinavian legal philosophy has almost exclusively been realistic in that sense since the beginning of this century.

But legal realism can also mean that court practice and legal science must pay regard to practical considerations of social *utility* in interpreting the legal material and ordering it in a system of rules. Legal decisions are taken as illustrations of such practical needs, and court practice on its side is guided by the analysis of such reasons by legal theory. In this respect there is a long tradition in Scandinavian legal theory especially in Denmark and Norway for legal realism. (Nordic realism).

Legal realism can also be conceived as a *theory of cognition* meaning that only real entities in the empirical world can be rationally conceived whereas valuations and norms are beyond cognition and therefore have no real existence. In this respect legal norms do not exist so that the legal facts which can be studied are the human feelings of obligation; law is a socio-psychological fact. (Scandinavian realism).

Legal realism can also be a *theory of science*. Logical positivism (not the same as legal positivism) is a realistic theory of science assuming that science only deals with assertions which can be verified pointing to data which correspond with the content of the assertions. Assertions of a legal norm can be verified by pointing to a higher norm from which it derives its validity (Kelsen), or by pointing to a corresponding behaviour or feeling of obligation (Ross).

Legal realism can finally mean that law is identical with what the Courts actually do, and that lawyers in any individual case must make prophecies about what the judge is likely to do taking all circumstances into consideration, as psychological motives. (American realism and partly Ross).

Sources of Law

To understand the above-mentioned relationship between »Scandinavian« and »Nordic« realism it is necessary to make a short historical outline. From ancient times there has existed a close political, legal and cultural co-operation between on the one hand Denmark and Norway, which were united from 1397 to 1814, and on the other hand between Sweden and Finland, which were united until 1809.

A common basis of the development within law[3] in all the Nordic countries, Iceland included, is found in the so-called »landskabslove« (provincial laws) from the 12th and the 13th centuries containing records of an older customary law with substantial common features. Late codifications (Danske Lov 1683, Norske Lov 1687, Svenske Lov 1734) are to a considerable extent conservative compilations of the rules of the provincial laws supplemented by the successive laws of posterity. Real, comprehensive codifications in a modern European sense were never introduced in the Nordic countries. On the other hand particular law reforms were introduced in each individual field from the end of the 19th century partially on a common Nordic basis. From 1872 Nordic »jurists' meetings« were held at regular intervals. Since 1953 »Nordisk Råd« (The Nordic Council) has been a consultative body for Nordic parliamentarians, and at regular intervals the Nordic ministers of justice meet to discuss common problems concerning legislation.

The lack of codification, on the other hand, was in favour of a further development of the antiquated and incomplete law material through theory and legal usage. Even though Samuel Pufendorf lived and acted in Sweden for twenty years from 1668, the rationalist natural law did not gain a footing in legal usage - and later in legal theory - until the 18th century.[4] However, a real, independent legal philosophy and legal science did not exist until the 19th century.

Nordic Realism. A. S. Ørsted

The Danish lawyer and politician *A. S. Ørsted* (1778-1860) is generally considered to be the father of Danish-Norwegian legal science.[5] He was influenced - like von Savigny - by Kant's critical philosophy, and he therefore rejected the rationalist natural law theory and favoured a positive and realistic jurisprudence. While von Savigny pointed out the spirit of the people and history as the source of law, Ørsted - like *Montesquieu* - referred to »the nature of things« (»nature des choses«, »Natur der Sache«) as the subsidiary, supplementing source of law. The concrete social conditions and common sense are the basis necessary for the right supplementing of the law and for the right legal policy. While *Jeremy Bentham* pointed out public utility as the purpose of the law, Ørsted referred to the »public benefit«.[6]

As already mentioned, Montesquieu assumed that there existed »rapports nécessaires« between »les choses« and »des lois«, i.e. necessary connections among the natural phenomena and between these and the social laws. Kant, however, divided the world into »the realm of necessity«, the world of nature, which presupposes the law of causation, and »the realm of freedom«, the spiritual world, which presupposes the law of responsibility. In this way Kant managed to combine empiricism with rationalism: on the one hand he had to agree with Hume that the law of causation cannot be proved empirically, but on the other hand he found that our apparatus of cognition cannot function without such ideas as time, space and causation. What is beyond cognition, »das Ding an sich«, can be reached only by means of intuition.

In contrast to Montesquieu, Kant - as mentioned - did not find that there existed a necessary connection between cognition and valuation. On the contrary the concept of responsibility had to imply the freedom of the will, which makes it impossible to infer an »is« from an »ought«.

Thus, Kant on the one hand separated »thought« (idea) and »reality«, and on the other limited cognition to the part of reality which corresponded with the idea, whereas Hegel went all out identifying reason with reality, which was considered to be constituted of and by the idea, which is also concretized in actual morality and law.

It is clear that Ørsted, like Montesquieu and Bentham, built upon an empirical theory of cognition and a realistic theory of law although he never gave up his religious belief. Neither Montesquieu nor Bentham[7] could take into consideration Kant's fundamental criticism of cognition, which maintained that it is not possible to deduce moral and legal laws from natural laws. Therefore, in his sociological theory Montesquieu could assume that there are certain »rapports necessaires« deciding divines, social and natural laws; and from his psychological theory that human beings are in fact in search of happiness Bentham could conclude that happiness therefore ought to be the aim.

However, Ørsted not only knew Kant's philosophy, but he even began his scientific work by defending Kant's moral and legal philosophy. Later on he rejected it, because it - in his opinion - remained too abstract. He then for some time subscribed to Fichte's theory, but repudiated it, as it developed in a speculative and systematizing direction, like the theories of Schelling and Hegel. Especially because he had to continue his practical career as a lawyer, a judge and a politician, he gave up philosophy and concentrated on his activities concerning legal dogmatism and legal politics. He found a sample of the »public benefit« in the *interplay between theory and practice*[8] and initiated the publication of law reports at regular intervals. If the study of and consideration for the social conditions (in Denmark-Norway) and the »public benefit« must be the foundation of the law, it is - in his opinion - not only for moral reasons but also because a *condition* of law being obeyed in the long run is that the population *accepts* it as being right.[9] As we shall see, this socio-psychological basis of the law is characteristic of the later »Nordic« and »Scandinavian« realism.

Ørsted's legal theory was adopted by the Norwegian professor *A. M. Schweigaard*, who in a well-known publication rejected the German legal philosophy from Wolff to von Savigny as vague, metaphysical and abstract. He emphasized Ørsted's analytical-descriptive method,[10] which became the norm of one of the movements in the later Norwegian legal theory and legal science.

Ørsted had no direct influence on Danish legal philosophy, which was represented by *C. Bornemann*.[11] Bornemann fully adopted Hegel's and Puchta's systematic-constructive school, which found the basis of the law in the development and manifestation of the spirit of the people in society, and attached only secondary importance to consideration of expediency. On the other hand Ørsted's activity had an extremely great influence on Danish legal practice and on certain parts of the dogmatic legal science.

Carl Goos[12] tried to combine Ørsted's practical realism with Bornemann's idealism. In his theory of unlawful actions, which contained elements of Kant's categorical imperative as well as of Stuart Mill's utilitarianism, Goos endeavoured to establish general rules of the limits of the liberty of action. These rules were laid down on the basis of a balancing of regard for the citizens' liberty of action on the one hand and of regard for the interests of society on the other. From the same considerations he defined the concept of subjective right as a »morally protected good«. Thus he arrived at a conception akin to Rudolph von Jhering's contemporary realistic definition of the right as a »legally protected interest«.

However, his dualistic legal philosophy was manifested in the distinction between the *purpose* of the law and the *grounds* of the law. The practical purpose of the criminal law is to prevent crimes, whereas its ethical grounds must be sought for in the punishment of the sane will. The grounds of the private law is - on the one hand - to be found in the »principle of person« and the »principle of will«, but - on the other hand - within the law of property this principle must compete with the »principle of society«. These grounds attaching decisive importance to the »interests of commerce« and to the »principle of reliance« result in the establishment of a »principle of expectation«, which competes with the »principle of will«. From the end of the last century this »principle of expectation and reliance« leads to the development of an objective law of contract and obligation in the uniform Scandinavian legislation.

Jhering's legal philosophy had a rather great direct influence on the two Norwegian jurists. *Francis Hagerup*[13] was influenced especially by the young Jhering's »constructive« and »natural scientific« method, whereas *Frederik Stang*[14] to a higher extent was influenced by the elder Jhering's »cultural scientific« legal conception. Hagerup - like the German »Interessenjurisprudenz« - insisted on a logical-systematic control of the practical balancing of interests derived from the purpose of the law. Stang (and the later *G. Astrup Hoel*)[15] - like the »German Freirechtsschule« and the »sociological theories« - endeavoured to develop a »cultural scientific« or »sociological« theory, which derived legal decisions from a direct balancing of the interests involved. This so-called »epic-lyrical« method has within modern Norwegian legal science competed with the above-mentioned empiric-analytical method.[16]

Legalism in Finland

Before I enter the discussion of the Dane *Viggo Bentzon*,[17] who was also influenced by Jhering's realistic theory of the balancing of interests, it is reasonable to pause for a moment to consider both the general development in Sweden and Finland and the general international current within philosophy around the turn of the century. For various reasons the realist current penetrated Swedish and Finnish legal philosophy later than elsewhere. Well into the 20th century the legal philosophy in Sweden and Finland was dominated first by movements related to natural law and later by idealistic movements, which were characterized by a strict conceptual formalism. One explanation is that industrial development and urbanization began later in these two countries; another explanation is that there were - especially in Finland - political reasons for maintaining a legalistic attitude towards Tsarist Russia, which, as mentioned, had political control in Finland from 1809 to 1918. As we shall see, realist legal science was introduced in Sweden as early as the 1920s and especially in the 1930s, whereas Danish-Norwegian and Swedish realism, as mentioned had only a limited influence on Finnish legal philosophy and legal science. The same was true of Jhering's theory of interest as well as of the »Freirechts«-movement. It was not until after World War II that Finnish legal science was able to free itself from the legalistic tradition, and it was rather analytic-hermeneutic than realistic movements which inspired the legal theorists, even though social sociological as well as Marxist elements formed part of the development; *Otto Brusiin, G. H. von Wright* and *Kaarle Makkonen* have anticipated and played an important part in this development.[18]

Cognition and Valuation

At the turn of the century the general rejection of the idealistic philosophy of cognition and moral philosophy all over the Western World had an influence on Viggo Bentzon's conception and therefore also on »Nordic realism« as well as on Swedish legal philosophy, which till then had been dominated by the general continental natural-law-systems in the 18th century and by the German idealistic »Begriffsjurisprudenz« in the 19th century, but which at the beginning of the 20th century developed »Scandinavian realism«.

That turn in philosophy gave rise to a coincident dispute at several places in the world. Rationalism was replaced by irrationalism or voluntarism, which emphasized intuition as the tool to establish the connection between the »objective« reality and the »objective« system of value, in which reason cannot obtain an insight, as reality and values are not structuralized in accordance with thought (idea) and language.

Even though *Henri Bergson*'s intuitionism was of a doubtful nature it influenced the contemporary conception of the relationship between subject and object and between cognition and valuation.[19] There had so to speak been a change of paradigm[20] in the philosophical and legal-theoretical debate, a change bearing on the progress of psychology which had resulted in a change of the conception of mental processes. Irrational feelings were preferred to rational thoughts, decisions to conclusions, motives to grounds. In this respect *William James* had a great international importance, when he strengthened the interest in psychology, the science of religion, and an intuitionistic-pragmatic theory of cognition.[21]

Edmund Husserl's phenomenology and hermeneutic were based on the condition that he who recognized by means of intuition can obtain a direct insight into the nature of things without using the rational apparatus of cognition, and that this insight can be achieved in an »objective hierarchy of value«.[22]

Even the German »Freirechtsschule« had - as mentioned - completely rejected the idea that the judicial decision or the application of the law is a logical conclusion; as reality is not constituted logically, either in the form of the projection of cognition, »Natur der Sache« (Kant), or through the rational logic of things, »sachlogische Strukturen« (Hegel), the judicial decision cannot be the result of a logical-deductive operation from an exhaustive legal system, but must be a decision, creating law, governed by intuition and the concept of justice. Later on the legal theory in Germany developed the so-called »Interessenjurisprudenz«, a teleological theory of interpretation and application, which on the basis of an analysis of the purpose of the law will find some guidelines for the valuations.[23]

A group of academics in the U.S.A. - one of them being *Oliver Wendell Holmes* - developed a pragmatic philosophy, which also assumes that »facts« exist prior to cognition, and that the »truth«, of statements about facts as well as of values, depends on their »use«.[24] The great problem of phenomenology as well as of pragmatism is to select and describe »facts« in relation to the intentional or instrumental values which depend on a kind of »consensus«.

The Englishman *G. E. Moore* also makes this anti-transcendental search back to things as they are from the common-sense-assumption that they exist prior to cognition. Thus, he denies that existence is identical with cognition,[25] and in his contemporary »Principia Ethica« he disputes the possibility of defining »good« as an abstraction because it is not an attribute of things. However, this does not mean that »good« does not exist, or that it is a subjective concept. Moore himself found that values are objective, but indefinable, and therefore they cannot be derived from scientific cognition. On the other hand our intuition enables us to apprehend »good«, »God«, and other high values.

Scandinavian Realism. Axel Hägerström

Some years later the Swede *Axel Hägerström*[26] initiated his campaign against the idealistic and transcendental philosophy. He claimed - like the above-mentioned philosophers - that things exist prior to and independently of cognition, which, on the other hand, can have only the physical world as its objects. As valuations are not attributes of things, but subjective feelings, objective cognition cannot think in norms, but only about norms, and neither can it deal with »metaphysical« phenomena like God, chimaeras, and other super-natural things.

It was this »realistic« and »value-nihilistic« cognitive and moral philosophy, which came to dominate Swedish legal philosophy in the subsequent period. Most consistent was *Vilhelm Lundstedt*,[27] who deprived legal science of its scientific character as a dogmatic-exegetic discipline; he insisted on »public utility« as the only realistic guide to the application of law.[28] The somewhat younger *Karl Olivecrona*[29] did not adopt the radical idea, but maintained, however, the »realistic« foundation of law. He considered law as a socio-psychological fact, »independent imperatives« motivating and internalizing the norms in the citizens. Like the legal philosophy in the Socialist countries, »Scandinavian realism« attached great importance on the pedagogical and internalizing element of rules of law.

Logical Empiricism. Alf Ross

These philosophical and legal ideas were prevalent when *Viggo Bentzon* in 1914 published his paper »Skøn og Regel«, in which he in an introductory note refers to Bergson's intuitionism as an important source of inspiration. As mentioned he had already published a textbook on jurisprudence (1904) and on the sources of law (1905), in which he had adopted Ørsted's realism and rejected Goos' attempt to combine practical realism with a theoretical idealism. Especially Bentzon had advocated a »descriptive« source-of-law theory, which took as its starting point the judges' actual grounds for their decisions, but now abandoned this »freirechtliche« point of view in favour of the conception that the judicial decision in the concrete case has to be made on the basis of a balancing of regard for the concrete justice and the »factual considerations« on the one hand and regard for the fact that the decision can serve as a guide to future decisions on the other. »The estimate must have its place, but the rule must not be disregarded«.[30]

Within modern Danish legal philosophy *Knud Illum* has most markedly carried on the realistic tradition initiated by Ørsted and Bentzon. In his book »Lov og Ret« (1945) Illum adheres to the interplay of legal theory and legal practice, considering »the general sense of justice« as the basis of law. According to Illum this general sense of justice is expressed especially in »the jurist's ideology«, whereas *Alf Ross* finds the criterion of »valid law« in »the judge's ideology«.[31]

It was Alf Ross who became particularly well-known abroad. As mentioned, Ross cannot directly be grouped among the representatives of »Scandinavian realism«. In the preface of the Danish version of his book »Ret og Retfærdighed«

(1953)[32)] Ross refers to his three teachers: Viggo Bentzon, Hans Kelsen, and Axel Hägerström. His first book »Theorie der Rechtsquellen« (1929) was influenced by Hans Kelsen's »Reine Rechtslehre«, the formal idealism of which he adopted. His second book »Kritik der sogenannten praktischen Erkenntnis« (1933) was inspired by Hägerström, and in his third book »Virkelighed og Gyldighed« (1934),[33)] which was inspired by Bentzon, he adopted an extreme realism, in so far as he considers law as a »phenomenon« and the judicial decision as a »psychological process of motivation«. In his chief work »On Law and Justice« Ross combines these two aspects and considers law as a combination of »legal ideological« and »empirical« phenomena.[34)] Law is the superindividual normative ideology which inspires the judges of a given society; but an insight in this ideology can be obtained only through the judges' normative grounds for the decisions. Ross now distinguishes between the actual psychological process of motivation leading to the decisions and the normative grounds indicating the rules, which the judge feels that he is bound to follow.[35)]

Ross himself protested with justice against his being identified with the behaviouristic attitude of »American realism«. He claimed - like the British analytical legal philosophy - that »law« implies obligations. But while Herbert Hart, for instance, considers »obligation« to be a logical category, »obligation« in Ross' opinion is a real phenomenon, a feeling of being obliged. His theory is - like Olivecrona's and Illum's theories - what he himself calls an *ideological realism*.[36)]

However, Ross is not himself blameless in this mistake, as his conception of law can be understood only as part of his conception of science or theory of science. Here it is important to establish that »On Law and Justice« is a book on *legal science*, and the theory of science that he adopts is *logical empiricism*,[37)] and not the »Uppsala-philosophy«, which is a general theory of cognition. According to logical empiricism a scientific statement is either true or false, if it states something about reality, which so to speak is reflected in our consciousness. Therefore, statements can be verified by comparing the linguistic content with the results of measurement defining the conditions of the truth. In contrast to »Scandinavian realism« not only objects in time and space are »real«, but also statements about »positive« norms and mathematical-logical coherences can be true. On the other hand, valuations are - also according to this theory - without »semantic reference«, just as statements about God and other »metaphysical« phenomena cannot be the subject of scientific discussion.

The difficulties of a logical-empirical verification of statements about »valid Danish law« are due to the uncertain instrument of verification. As mentioned, Illum refers to the general jurist's ideology as the criterion of the »validity« of the law, whereas Ross refers to the judge's ideology. Ross' opinion is a consequence

of his thesis that law implies the use of the machinery of power of society. Therefore, the rules of law are ultimately considered as directives to legal authorities to
sanction violations of the citizens' *norms of conduct*, which on the other hand are
considered to be a reflex of the *norms of competence* of the authorities.[38] Therefore
the process of verification will consist in calculations of the probability of the
courts' making a given norm the basis of a hypothetic future case.[39] According
to this criterion several rules of law will be unverifiable, as there would be no judicial decision, but in practice it is undoubtedly true that the »calculation of
probability«, which the lawyer pretends to make, is in fact a direct valuation of
the »validity« of the rule. Add to this - as it has also been objected - that the
condition of anybody being able to make a calculation of probability and of the
rules of law being able to »function as a scheme of interpretation« for the machinery of justice is the very fact that the citizens, like the judge, have an insight into
the rules.

Not only does the instrument of verification veil this element in the concept of
law, but it even becomes unnecessary, as both lawyers and judges have to find
the solution on the basis of the same sources and by means of the same method.
One difficulty is that the »common ideology of judges« , which is the criterion of
»valid law«, is one of these »superindividual« and consequently »metaphysical«
phenomena, which cannot be verified according to the chosen theory of science.
Another difficulty is that a real insight into »law« = »ideology« can be obtained
only by reading the grounds for the judgments, while on the other hand from his
value-nihilistic point of view Ross cannot be sure that the given grounds correspond to the real motives, as the grounds can be »transcendental nonsense« (Felix Cohen). Difficulties arise for the theory of the sources of law as well: Ross,
clearly, recognizes the existence of binding sources of law, but on the other hand
includes »the ideology of the sources of law« under »the ideology of law«, which,
as already mentioned, is identical with the judges' feeling of being bound, and
which only appears in the grounds for the judgments. So we end up with a »descriptive« theory of the sources of law, and therefore - as stressed by Illum - the
grounds for the judgments cannot be criticized.[40]

Sociology of Law

Above have been mentioned some of the difficulties, which arise when Ross tries
to combine an »ideological« (psychological) theory of law with a »sociological«
theory of law. Already at an early stage the Norwegian *Vilh. Aubert* called attention to the fact that the Uppsala-philosophy in principle had to result in a grad-
ual change of the science of law into a sociology of law,[41] and Aubert and his
colleague *Torstein Eckhoff* also founded the Nordic sociology of law.[42]

Pluralism

Now, I have described the lines of »Nordic« and »Scandinavian« realism up to the present time and indicated the criticism, which also internally in Scandinavia has been put forward against their consequences. I suppose the younger generation has preserved the »realistic« foundation,[43] inasmuch as this generation to a still higher degree has been occupied with the problem of the application of law in the widest sense, i.e. the analysis of the relation between the abstract rules of law and the concrete reality. Thus this is the problem of the judicial decision as well as of the dogmatics of law, as the purpose of the rules of law is to influence the social reality. In this respect the analytical philosophy of language created by Wittgenstein has exerted a great influence on the Nordic legal philosophers, especially in Finland,[44] but also the general hermeneutics derived from German philosophy has influenced Danish as well as Swedish legal philosophers.[45]

These theories have in common the rejection of the basic conditions of the logical empirical theory of science, i.e. the theory that »reality« is of such a »linguistic« structure that it can be »reflected« in our (linguistic) consciousness. This criticism results in the fact that »reality« cannot be described in an »objective« language, but instead has to be »qualified« linguistically, which is an act or the result of a decision, inasmuch as the language is intentional, i.e. meant to obtain certain purposes, and that our concepts therefore are loaded with value.

In the analysis of the problem of the application of law legal argumentation appears to be very important. »Teleological« as well as »pragmatical« elements combined with linguistic-logical and (legal) ideological arguments form part of this analysis. In modern moral philosophy it has been recognized that justice is a social value competing with the public utility.[46] In the attempt at filling the gap between cognition and valuation has been seen some tendencies derived from neo-natural law,[47] whereas others have found it possible to define the criteria of valuations so distinctly that they assume an »objective« character.[48] Some have stressed the more or less intersubjectivity of valuations, while others have made (legal) sociological analyses of the concept of justice.[49]

However, altogether there is in our time a pluralistic conception of legal philosophy, which results in the fact that logical,[50] analytical, system-theoretical,[51] and Marxist[52] theories can be found side by side with theories derived from neo-realism[53] and neo-natural law.[54]

Pluralis Juris

Personally I have developed what I have called a relationistic or pluralistic theory of law.[55] Law is not just a system of norms, a prediction of the behaviour of the authorities, commands to the authorities or the citizens, a legal concept, ideology, behaviour, sanctioned norms of conduct or custom. Law is all this and other things - at the same time. The different definitions select a single relation which is then hypostatized as »law«. But the different definitions are only models and analogies by which the special interest in cognition is expressed and by this often a further political interest.

It is without any doubt no coincidence that law in the socialist countries is defined in accordance with Hans Kelsen's view as commands of the state backed by threats and that legal science is only recognized as the theory of Law and State. On the other hand, it is equally obvious that sociological definitions like those of American realism and the German Niklas Luhman's system theory, according to which law is a rolling system of procedures by which social life is adapted to developing social needs, reflect the ideas of a market economy.

But also in the other cases definitions of law reflect the nature of the questions asked and to whom they are addressed. In authoritarian state definitions the state is, as mentioned, the legal actor, in Anglo-Saxon tradition the judges are usually regarded as the honoratiores whose actions are often identified with the law, whereas in Germany the legal professors have been regarded the authentic interpreters of law regarded as general concepts. It is quite clear that what advocates are interested in is the probable outcome of concrete cases, »the bad man's law«, but it is equally clear that from the judge's perspective definitions of that kind are not satisfactory, neither are definitions concerning his feelings of being obliged. To him law must be obligatory norms derived from recognized sources. The dogmatic legal theorist is interested in seeing law as binding rules which he interprets and integrates in a systematic context. Legal dogmatics is usually the most important part of legal science, because of its consultative function for legal practice. Therefore, extreme formalistic or sociological definitions and philosophies of law have not been of lasting importance.

Of course, Hans Kelsen's and Herbert Hart's formal-analytical philosophy of law like legal logic has been of great importance to the understanding of the structure of law. But by excluding valuations and pragmatic considerations from their analysis, they cannot produce a theory of legal decision and interpretation. The same is true of most so-called »realistic« theories, especially the Scandinavian realism. Therefore it is essential that legal philosophy deals with moral, economic and political values not only to provide legal dogmatics with a rational theory of argumentation and decision but also to involve itself in a dialogue with the other social sciences: anthropology, psychology, sociology, economy and political science, to contribute to the analysis of what is the »good society«. The long history of legal philosophy has developed an understanding of the importance of the function of what we call »justice« in competition with utility arguments, and how legal norms and expectations are necessary to cope with the central social task: to make the optimal distribution of freedom and security.

There also seems to be a dawning understanding within the social sciences that law is not only a plumbing or ambulance service designed to repair defects and deal with emergencies in the functioning of society, but a condition precedent for its organisation and functioning.

Notes

1) See, for instance *R. W. H. Dias*, Jurisprudence (4th ed, 1976) p. 639 ff; *Lord Lloyd of Hampstead*, Introduction to Jurisprudence (4th ed, 1979) Ch. 8; *Julius Stone*, Legal System and Lawyers' Reasonings (1964) p. 92-93; *Wolfgang Fikentscher*, Methoden des Rechts II (1975) p. 322 ff; *Alfred Verdross*, Abendländische Rechtsphilosophie (2. Aufl. 1965) p. 196 ff. See further *H.-H. Vogel*, Der skandinavische Rechtsrealismus (1972); *Stig Strömholm* and *H.-H. Vogel*, Le »Realisme Scandinave« dans la Philosophie du Droit (1975); *Enrico Pattaro*, Il Realismo Giuridico Scandinavo (1975); *Jes Bjarup*, Skandinavischer Realismus (1978); *Silvana Castignone*, Il Realismo Giuridico Scandinavo e Americano (1981); *Karl Olivecrona*, The Legal Theories of Axel Hägerström and Vilhelm Lundstedt, in: Scandinavian Studies in Law, 3 (1959) 125; *Folke Schmidt*, The Uppsala School of Legal Thinking, in: Scandinavian Studies in Law, 22 (1978) 149.

2) See my previous articles: Grundzüge der Entwicklung der skandinavischen Rechtswissenschaft, in: Juristenzeitung (1970) 529; Skandinavische Rectswissenschaft 1850-1950, in: Österreichische Zeitschrift für Öffentliches Recht, 27 (1976) 241; Legal Science during the Last Century, in: *Rotondi*, Inchiesti di Diritto Comparato, 6 (1976) 504; On Legal Theory in Denmark, in: *Enrico Pattaro*, Legal Philosophical Library: and International Bibliography of Philosophy and Theory of Law, Denmark (1980) p. 25 ff; Über die allgemeine Rechtslehre in Dänemark, in: Archiv für Rechts- und Sozialphilosophie (ARSP) Beiheft Neue Folge, Nr. 13 (1979) 25; Entwicklung und Methode des Privatrechts, in: *Stig Jørgensen*, Vertrag und Recht (1968) p. 49 ff; Die Bedeutung Jherings für die neuere skandinavische Rechtslehre, in: *F. Wieacker* und *Chr. Wollschläger*, Jherings Erbe (1970) p. 116 ff; Typologie und Realismus, in: Nachrichten der Akademie der Wissenschaften in Göttingen, I Philologisch-Historische Klasse (1971) Nr. 3, 17.

3) See to the following *Stig Jørgensen*, Traits Principaux de l'Evolution des Sources du Droit Danois, in: Revue Internationale de Droit Comparé (1971) 65.

4) Roman Law had at an earlier date been introduced in Sweden, which since the Thirty Years' War had controlled large possessions on the Continent. *Stig Jägerskiöld*, Roman Influence on Swedish Case Law, in Scandinavian Studies in Law, 11 (1967) 175.

5) See also *Stig Jørgensen*, Grundzüge ... (supra n. 3) and Vertrag und Recht (supra n. 3) p. 76; *Ditlev Tamm*, Anders Sandøe Ørsted and the Influence from Civil Law upon

Danish Private Law at the Beginning of the 19th Century, in: Scandinavian Studies in Law, 22 (1978) 243.

6) See *Stig Jørgensen,* Natural Law Today, in: Jørgensen, Values in Law: Ideas, Principles and Rules, (1978) p. 135 ff.

7) See *Jørgen Dalberg-Larsen,* Retsvidenskaben som samfundsvidenskab (with a German summary) (1977) p. 230. *A. S. Ørsted,* Af mit Livs og min Tids Historie (abbreviated ed. 1951) p. 126.

8) See *Stig Jørgensen,* Idealism and Realism in Jurisprudence, in: Values in Law (supra n. 7) p. 33.

9) *A. S. Ørsted,* Over de første Grundregler for Straffelovgivningen, in: Eunomia, 2 (1817).

10) Juridisk Tidsskrift, 23 (1834) p. 332.

11) See *Stig Jørgensen,* Grundzüge ... (supra n. 3) p. 531; same, Vertrag und Recht (supra n. 3) p. 78 ff.

12) *Stig Jørgensen,* Grundzüge ... (supra n. 3) p. 531; same, Vertrag und Recht (supra n. 3) p. 81.

13) *Stig Jørgensen,* in Jherings Erbe (supra n. 3) p. 123; same, Grundzüge ... (supra n. 3) p. 531.

14) *Stig Jørgensen,* in Jherings Erbe (supra n. 20) p. 123 ff; same, Grundzüge ... (supra n. 3) p. 532.

15) *Stig Jørgensen,* Grundzüge ... (supra n. 3) p. 533, same, in Jherings Erbe (supra n. 3) p. 122.

16) The former method is represented by among others Ragnar Knoph, Kirsten Anderson, and Carl Jacob Arnholm, and the latter by among others Per Augdal, Johs. Andenæs, and Sjur Brækhus. See *Stig Jørgensen,* Grundzüge ... (supra n. 3) p. 533.

17) *Stig Jørgensen,* Grundzüge ... (supra n. 3) p. 533; same, in Jherings Erbe (supra n. 3) p. 123.

18) See *Aulis Aarnio,* On Finnish Legal Theory in the 20th Century, in: Legal Points of View (1978) p. 1 ff; and *Hannu Tapani Klami,* Legal Philosophy in Finland (1982).

19) See *Karl Larenz,* Methodenlehre der Rechtswissenschaft (4. Aufl. 1979) p. 64; *Dieter v. Stephanitz,* Exakte Wissenschaft und Recht (1970) p. 214.

20) On this subject see *Thomas Kuhn,* The Structure of Scientific Revolutions (1967).

21) *William James,* Principles of Psychology (1981); same, The Varieties of Religious Experience (1902); same, Pragmatism (1907).

22) *Edmund Husserl,* Logische Untersuchungen (1901).

23) *Karl Larenz,* (supra n. 20) p. 64 ff and p. 406 ff.; *A. Kaufmann and W. Hassemer,* Einführung in Rechtsphilosophie und Rechtstheorie der Gegenwart (3. Aufl. 1981) p. 52 ff. and p. 94 ff.; *Heinrich Henkel,* Einführung in die Rechtsphilosophie (2. Aufl. 1977) p. 371 ff.; *Reinhold Zippelius,* Rechtsphilosophie (1982) p. 49 ff.

24) *John Dewey,* Studies in Logical Theory (1903); *William James,* Pragmatism (1907).

25) *G. E. Moore,* Refutation of Idealism (1903).

26) *Axel Hägerström,* Das Prinzip der Wissenschaft. Eine logischerkenntnistheoretische Untersuchung, in: Die Realität (1908).

27) *Vilhelm Lundstedt,* Die Unwissenschaftlichkeit der Rechtswissenschaft I-II (1932-1933), in: Legal Thinking Revised (1956).

28) See on the contemporary Danish jurist Fr. Vinding Kruse, *Stig Jørgensen*, in Jherings Erbe (supra n. 3) p. 124; same, Grundzüge ... (supra n. 3) p. 532.

29) *Karl Olivecrona*, Law as Fact (2nd ed. 1971).

30) *Viggo Bentzon*, who in note 1 of his book, Skøn og Regel (1914) refers to Henri Bergson's inspiration, was philosophically influenced by the book by the Danish philosopher *Harald Høffding*, Filosofiens Historie I-II (2. ed. 1903-1904), which took psychology as its starting point. In his publications Bentzon attaches importance to psychological features in man's identification of himself with the rules and their application, and to custom: »the criteria of the sources of law develop from legal usage«, he writes in his book Retskilderne (1905) p. 136 and p. 74, and in: Svensk Juristtidning (1929) p. 533 ff. He distinguishes between rules, for instance rules of law, which the courts must apply, and other rules - including custom and usage - which the courts may apply (Retskilderne, p. 76 and p. 82).

31) See *Alf Ross*, Some Reflections on the Method of Legal Science and on Legal Reasoning, in: Scandinavian Studies in Law, 12 (1968) 49.

32) The English version of *Alf Ross'* book On Law and Justice (1958) mentions in its preface only Kelsen and Hägerström. Ross mentions that from Kelsen he has learned logical conclusion, from Hägerström about the emptiness of moral methaphysics and from Bentzon a realistic juridical method.

33) English version: Towards a Realistic Jurisprudence (1946).

34) See to the following Ch. 1-2 of On Law and Justice. In the Danish version of the book (p. 41, note 1) Ross admits that in his Virkelighed og Gyldighed (Towards a realistic Jurisprudence) he one-sidedly defined law as a real phenomenon. He refers to the review (in Tidsskrift for Rettsvitenskap (1952) 38 (58)) by the Norwegian philosopher Harald Ofstad as his source of inspiration to the conception that law is idea as well as phenomenon.

35) *Alf Ross*, On Law and Justice (supra n. 33) p. 34 ff., p. 68.

36) *Alf Ross*, On Law and Justice (supra n. 33) p. 70 ff. (p. 71, note 1); although Ross himself repudiated this name (l.c. p. 72). In his later book: Directives and Norms (1968) Ross develops his theory still further, and recognizes that »obligation« has a purely logical side as well.

37) *Alf Ross*, On Law and Justice (supra n. 33) p. 38 ff.

38) *Alf Ross*, On Law and Justice (supra n. 33) p. 32 ff.

39) *Alf Ross*, On Law and Justice (supra n. 33) p. 40 ff.

40) See *Stig Jørgensen*, Values in Law, (supra n. 7) p. 151 ff. and p. 9 ff., in: ARSP (supra n. 3) p. 30; same, Die rechtliche Entscheidung und ihre Begründung, in: Rhetorische Rechtstheorie (1982) p. 337.

41) Tidsskrift for Rettsvitenskap (1943) p. 174 ff.

42) *Torstein Eckhoff and Knut Sveri*, En lov i søkelyset (1952); *Vilh. Aubert*, Rettssosiologi (1968); *Torstein Eckhoff*, Justice (1974); *Theodor Geiger* worked in Denmark in the 1940s and wrote here among other things Vorstudien zu einer Soziologie des Rechts (1947).

43) *A. Peczenik*, Juridikens metodproblem (1974).

44) *Aulis Aarnio*, On Legal Reasoning (1977); same, Denkweisen der Rechtswissenschaft (1979); see also *Kaarle Makkonen*, Zur Problematik der juridischen Entscheidung

(1965); see also *Otto Brusiin*, Über die Objektivität der Rechtsprechung (1949); see also *Preben Stuer Lauridsen*, Retspolitisk argumentation (1974); same, Retslæren (1977).

45) *Stig Jørgensen*, Law and Society (Recht und Gesellschaft (1971)); same, Values in Law (supra n. 7) same, Norm und Wirklichkeit, in: Rechtstheorie (1971) p. 1 ff.; same, Hermeneutik und Auslegung, in: Rechtstheorie (1978) p. 63 ff.; *Hannu Tapani Klami*, Confessiones Methodologicae (1981); *Stig Strömholm*, Allgemeine Rechtslehre (1976).

46) See *Stig Jørgensen*, (supra n. 46); same, Pluralis Juris: Towards a Relativistic Theory of Law. Acta Jutlandica LVI (Aarhus, 1982); see also *Torstein Eckhoff*, (supra n. 43).

47) *Frede Castberg*, Forelesninger over Rettsfilosofi (1965), in which the author points out that human rights and justice must be respected by a valid legal system (p. 25 ff.); a new cultural legal idealism has been formulated by *Jacob Sundberg*, Från Eddan till Ekelöf (1978).

48) *Nils Jareborg*, Värderingar (1975).

49) *Torstein Eckhoff*, (supra n. 43).

50) *C. H. von Wright*, Handlung, Norm and Intention (1977); *Stig Kanger*, Law and Logic, in: Theoria (1972) p. 105 ff.; *Stig Jørgensen*, Pluralis Juris (supra n. 47).

51) *Torstein Eckhoff and Nils Kr. Sundby*, Rettssystemer (1976).

52) *Per Eklund*, Rätten i klasskampen (1974); *Lars D. Eriksson*, Marxistisk teori och rättsvetenskap (1980).

53) *Stig Strömholm*, (supra n. 46); *A. Peczenik*, (supra n. 44); *Preben Stuer Lauridsen*, (supra n. 45); *Stig Jørgensen*, (supra n. 46).

54) *Jacob Sundberg*, (supra n. 48).

55) *Stig Jørgensen*, Pluralis Juris (supra n. 47); same, Law and Society (supra n. 46) Ch. 1.

Pluralis Juris

The title »Pluralis Juris« may seem a bit confusing, but it is at the same time the title of a little booklet, which I published recently. The direct translation of the title would undoubtedly be plurality of law. You may then ask why I have chosen to use a Latin form and not plain English. You must believe me when I say that it is not exclusively reflecting academic snobbery, but at least two other regards. The title is meant to be a little striking, so that it makes people notice and re-member and sometimes even think about the meaning of the title. This purpose you will easier achieve when the title is additionally a little ambiguous. As I men-tioned before the plain meaning of the title be something like the plurality of law. There might be another nuance or an alternative interpretation which concurs with my idea of connection between law and politics. Pluralis juris can mean also: majority for the law or put in another way that law in our part of the world is a reflection of a democratic political system, and on the other hand that law is the device for governing a pluralistic society.

To begin at the beginning it is a substantial idea of my book that law like any other phenomenon in reality cannot be defined in one and only one way. Any definition which is a mental construct isolating particular elements of the phen-omenon and putting them together according to criteria in a preexisting mental system is in the end governed by some general or special cognition interest. Defi-nitions are tools for the mental activity called science, the purpose of which is to increase the knowledge of man. Definitions or concepts are abstractions of some part of reality, abstractions which make it possible for man to communicate in a symbolic way, information from one individual to another. Concepts may be vague and open-ended, the so-called type-concepts, which are commonly used in everyday language and in the social sciences. In mathematics and natural sciences deliminating concepts or definitions are usually contrary to type-con-cepts which are characterized by the intensity of elements. The deliminating con-cepts or definitions are characterized by exact numbers and relations between the elements. Of course the use of deliminating concepts makes it possible to derive exact conclusions and to predict process consequences according to the general logical and scientific system according to which they are defined. But of course such certainties are achieved at the expense of plasticity. If you have defined man according to an anatomical system you cannot at the same time understand man as a biological or physiological phenomenon and not at all as a social or cultural creature. But even if you have chosen to talk about phenomena according to one system of criteria it may be difficult to operate with deliminating concepts due to the general vagueness of the language. Especially sciences, which are dealing with daily life, the so-called social sciences in general and legal science in particular, you have to deal with concepts which are already existing in general language and in the legal system. Therefore the interpretation of law in legal science is dealing with concepts which have an ordinary or general linguistic meaning which is not deliminated, for instance wood, house, public street, negligence, fraud and so on. We must never forget that legal rules are not theoretical expressions, assertions or allegations neither are they expressions of art which may be interpreted individually. But legal rules are meant to affect reality by influencing the minds of the population conveying a meaning which is not understood if it does not refer to the concepts which are already in operation in the minds of the addressees. It is generally assumed that the ambiguity of the concepts in the language is the necessary preconditions for the economy of speech. If concepts could not be used in a variety of different meanings the languages had to contain many times as many words and concepts as they already do. Vagueness is so to speak a necessary aspect of language so that context, interest and purpose decide which interpretation of the concepts is valid in the given speach act.

It is common knowledge for everybody today that science is not and cannot be entirely objective. Science must be dependent on a meta-science or philosophy of science which lies behind science as a guiding principle. What is known as meta-science does not constitute a subject of its own but is the science of science. Like philosophy it deals with the basis of science, but it does not, however, treat the question of cognition as such as an essential problem but rather focuses on the methods applied by science. The ideal of the so-called logical-empiristic or positivistic meta-science of the Vienna circle, which dominated from the 1920s to the 1950s, was that science be value-free. But as we have already mentioned this is an ideal which has not the same credibility after the progress of linguistic analyses of the last decades. We have always known that there has been so to speak built in a moral demand to science in the demand for truth. But truth is not only a moral demand but also a condition of scientific communication and collaboration. The above-mentioned positivism of the Vienna circle had the superior purpose of keeping science free from political, ideological and religious usurpation in the growing totalitarian tendencies in Europe. In the centre of the theory was the linguistic expression. Only statements, i.e. assertions, which can be empirically verified or which are analytically, i.e. logically, self-evident can be accepted as scientific statements. Metaphysical assertions, which cannot be verified, and statements containing evaluations are of no scientific relevance. These demands on science have been applied with great success in mathematics and the natural sciences since the days of Descartes and Galileo. The new practice is to make the same demands for objectivity on other sciences: the social sciences and the humanities.

In opposition to positivism various movements among the cultural sciences have framed a hermeneutic-dialectical or critical-scientific ideal. The point of departure in recent times has to be looked for in the French and German phenomenology of the 1930s and the 1940s. To the functional descriptions of its objects adhered to by positivism Heidigger raised the objection that any human activity is based on a conscious or unconscious intentionality. Human conduct is purposive. If therefore science confines itself to a description of human activity, that description will at most be a very imperfect one. It will be able only to answer the question »how« and not the question »why«. Science cannot deal scientifically with the interpretation of the meaning of the activity. Moreover linguistic theory acknowledges that language is in itself filled with a hidden meaning and interpretation of reality. It is impossible to apply a linguistic expression without at the same time speaking intentionally. You cannot for instance mention the word »table« in a sentence without having also said something about the use of this piece of furniture. When analysing other words, concepts and sentences one must end up with a theoretical assumption that it is impossible to pronounce on anything whatever without having a preconceived opinion of it. This is the so-called hermeneutic circle. Another branch of phenomenology, the so-called structuralism or semiology, seems to regard reality as a reflection of linguistic structures. A more relevant observation is perhaps the underlining by the ideology-critical Frankfurt School of the fact that the basis of cognition is interest. The problem that has to be solved is that of finding out what factors determine our choice of value-concepts in the formation of theories as well as ideologies. It seems natural to stress on anthropology or human biology, the fact that man is created in such a way that he is able to feel certain needs and consequently to have certain interests.

As a matter of fact Immanuel Kant's theory of cognition underlined in principle the limits, which are set to cognition by the human apparatus of cognition.

To this must be added that biological assumption of the influence of our needs on the direction of our interests and so on our interest in the direction of cognition. It has already been mentioned that cognition is an activity, which has an intellectual and therefore a linguistic character. Our cognition is so to speak limited by our linguistic capacity. What cannot be formulated in language cannot easily be made the object of cognition. The analytical philosophy of language has been occupied especially with analysing everyday language on the assumption that it contains the culture or heritage of mankind, which is held to have settled into the language through the process of culture and consequently of cognition. This is exactly what the so-called hermeneutic science claims: that there is so to speak no possibility of cognition and science without regard to the cultural system and tradition lying behind the actual culture and the purposes and goals of man according to his cultural background.

I have tried to illustrate the general situation of science directly by our abilities and interests with the parable of the elephant. In doing this I was inspired by an article by the American legal philosopher Felix Cohen, who in his article »Field Theory and Judicial Logic« in the Yale Law Journal, No. 59, 1950, p. 238, took his starting point in Einstein's relativity theory and transferred to legal philosophy the insight of this theory that cognition depends on perspective and instrument: »Rather does the field concept, which recognizes the limited and relative validity of many apparently conflicting views in the practical struggles of the law court and market place, point to the possibility that many conflicting schools of jurisprudence may all be true and valid differing and limited perspectives and regions.«

But after having published my booklet my learned colleague professor Manfred Rehbinder from Zürich has corrected me referring to his edition of Karl Llewellyn's lectures on legal theory in Dresden in 1931 »Rechtsleben und Gesellschaft« from 1977, p. 42, from which Felix Cohen might have borrowed his elephant parable, which runs as follow: Seven blind sages were given the task of defining an elephant. One found that the elephant was a wall, another that it was a pillar, the third called it a snake, the fourth a spear, while number five and six felt certain that it was a whip and a big leaf respectively. The seventh was convinced of its being a thunderstorm.

The parable point to the fact that our cognition is fragmentary delimited by our ability to grasp reality by the instrument we are using in the cognitive progress and by the interests, which are lying behind the questions we put. It is obvious that we do not get an answer to questions that we have not yet put, and we get the answers that our instruments are capable of providing. That does not mean, however, that the outcome of the cognition process is incorrect. It just means that one gets only a variety of true answers and that the truth has many faces.

A theory cannot be true as such but it can be of use as a description of certain phenomena. At least the theory cannot be true unless truth is defined as the fact that the theory is not at variance with reality. One cannot exclude the possibility that reality may be described just as truly in another way. One of the classic examples is the description of light as either waves or particles. Both are equally true according to the purpose of the description to be made and the methods used to verify the theory.

This pluralistic or relativistic view of science lies behind the anecdote, which illustrates the dependence of science upon purposes and possibilities. Because of such a dependence scientific descriptions and methods must be in accordance with the varying purposes of science, and a theory, therefore, that fails when confronted with a special problem cannot claim to be true, that means to contain a sufficiently comprehensive description. On the other hand the critic needs no other reason for his criticism than the fact that the theory is unable to cover a single isolated case.

History knows examples enough that science in general or special sciences have been forced to change their course and take another direction than forward. That is why the history of ideas or civilization is as popular with some as it is heretical with others. Critical or macro-oriented scientists are for it, while steady and micro-oriented researchers are against it. The distaste for the comparative perspective laid upon the sciences by the history of ideas is understandable considering the amount of dilettantism and sciolism displayed in the latest twenty years under the name of science-criticism, especially by the so-called Marxists. Nevertheless the comparative view is an important corrective to any kind of dogmatism.

The science of any period in history of course is part of the culture of that period and must be understood as such. The oldest science was partly determined by a religious purpose. But when the Greeks founded the real science in a rational search for eternity in the changeable world, they were led by the basic idea that everything had a purpose. Thus science becomes teleological, and the social science is founded on the idea that reasonable insight in the essence of man and the source of natural law must lead to the correct acting. The medieval social science, which to a great extent is identical with the moral philosophy of the church, very easily took over this teleological view of science and replaced the essence of man by the will of God, so that the natural law coincided with the church law.

The transmission of Aristotle's writings from the Arabs to the European culture in the 12th century marked the beginning of a scientific renaissance. This was especially the case within the moral legal sciences as at the same time a copy of the classical Roman law, the Digesta, was found. However, mathematics and logic are still important patterns of the other sciences in the efforts to establish an uncontradictory and coherent system of doctrine. This is done in the form of questiones and answered by means of argumenta pro et contra taken from the Holy Bible, Aristotle and the Digesta. The scientific perspective, however, was altered with the world picture, which shifted from the Earth as a central body of the Universe common to the Bible and the Greek, to the idea of the sun as a centre of a planet system. It was Copernicus who proved mathematically that the Earth was able to revolve around the sun but it was Galileo, who was sentenced for heresy by the church when he wanted to draw the physical consequences of this fact in the beginning of the 17th century. According to Galileo's functional conception of sciences speculations regarding the essence of things were replaced by quantitative measurements and research regarding course and effect, and this method was also adapted by other sciences. By and by the rationalist natural law developed a doctrine of an eternal and unchangeable system of rights and duties and set a moral and legal science of universal validity beside the imperfect positive law. The late 18th century philosophers, especially Hume and Kant, denied the possibility of gaining an insight in the eternally good and right things by means of speculation, and the 19th century science was characterized on the whole by the industrialization and the evolutionism. While mathematics was a paradigm of the sciences in the Middle Ages, and physics and astronomy of the Renaissance, sciences of electricity, chemistry and biology became the paradigms of the 19th century with their process-orientation. The cultural sciences were dominated by historicism and evolution and the legal science developed a new formalism and a legal positivism derived from a limited set of principles or ideas based upon the conditions of national human life. But later on in the 19th century it became clear that political and legal acts are governed by purposes and interests. Rudolf Jhering reveals the fact that legal rules are the result of the political power struggle. By the turn of the century we are approaching the contemporary dissolution of the world picture and the unity of science. The relativity theory states that there exists no unambiguous and clear cosmology but that the description of the phenomena depends on the measuring instruments and so on purposes and interests. The legal science developed a number of so-called realistic and analytical theories which have one characteristic in common: each of them underlines a specific aspect of the function of law.

The short raid through the history of science illustrates the dependence of science upon the horizon of understanding and the cognition interest of its time. A reflection on the various purposes or functions of law makes it equally clear that it will not be possible to maintain a monistic conception of law. Like Kuhn one might speak of various paradigms being the methodical traits generally accepted by the pursuers of the specific sciences at a given time and in doing so indicate the method to be used according to the purposes of its time. One might also prefer not to choose a specific paradigm for the legal science. In order to avoid the fallacies invariably accompanying any dogmatics that magnifies one out of more scientific aims into *the* aim, and so to speak takes the object of science to be monistic, one might try to adopt a pluralistic point of view on legal science.

The point of what I have said about science in general is that law and legal science are phenomena of the history of culture, which makes it natural to look upon legal science as part of the comprehensive scientific universe being at the service of the interests in power at the time in question.

The law has always had different functions, some of which are original while others have been added as society grew more and more complex.

It is necessary to look upon law from a functional point of view to avoid the risk of defining away important functions from the legal science. A comparative method in the widest sense, that means vertical as well as horizontal, historical as well as international or intersystematic, must necessarily be functional. It does not make sense to compare institutions at different times or places, which do not have the same function just as it would be meaningless to separate different institutions, which have the same function totally or partly. For cultures which are closely related in time or contents there will be no great difficulties, but the difficulties will increase according to the distance in these respects.

As regards the legal science it is an obvious absurdity to define law in general in relation to the modern political institutions and afterwards to maintain that past and present so-called primitive societies with none of these institutions have or have had no legal rules either. For example it has been a common practice in connection with the neo-positivist theory of science from the 1920s up till today to identify law and state, which has led to the result that many ethnologists dealing with pre-state societies have found themselves obliged to deny the existence of law in such societies. Likewise Karl Marx and the Marxists or some of them have prophesied the none-existence of law in the future Communist society where the state will wither away.

Peace and Order

Whenever people have formed a society there has been a need for means to secure peace with the outside world and order at home. In the latter respect it is important to develop mechanisms partly to prevent conflicts and partly to settle them. The history of law tells us about the family feuds of earlier times being replaced by »tings« and courts where conflicts are settled by means of generally accepted rules. Such rules in all probability have developed by and by through the settlement of various types of conflicts by mediation or arbitration.

The function of settling conflicts, however, is not the only function of law, and not the most important one either, although it must be presumed that the actual legal rules have developed from this function. The most important need of human societies is not the settlement but the prevention of conflicts, and this task is given the first rank among the functions of law and may be called its political function in the widest sense.

To this external or political aspect of society-preserving functions corresponds the general concept of public utility as the basic value or criterion for balancing the conflicting social interests. In primitive or poorly developed societies the conflict between individual and common interests is not apparent as the conception of man in these societies is collective, that means that the unit of societies is society itself and that the individuals are only fragments or parts of the totality.

In further developed societies, particularly in city-states or urbanized societies in general, emerges a conflict between the individual and the society as man is regarded as a mixture of individual and social elements. In the modern technological society with its mass production and mass consumption a new collective or Socialist conception of man has developed putting again the public utility on top of the hierarchy of values in society and deciding conflicts between individual and social interest in favour of the latter.

Corresponding to the above mentioned external viewpoint of law one can choose another viewpoint that deals with the internal functions of law or microfunction connected with internal considerations as the point of departure of individual evaluations and dispositions. Considerations of justice in the widest sense play an important part in this area. Formal and material expectations as to the consequences of one's own dispositions in relation to reactions of society and the surroundings lead to a certain degree of predictability which can be obtained in principle under any material system provided that it is formally governed by rules and not discretionary.

Formal Justice

The core of formal justice is the expectation that equal cases will be treated equally. In this sense the concept of equality is socially valuable and related to the rule of law.

Material Justice

Already Aristotle divided justice into two main types. On the one hand he points to the fact that *commutative justice* means that there must be equality between the tenders that individuals have to exchange between themselves and between the evil and the sanction which is laid upon the wrongdoer.

Aristotle recognizes that since the days of Solon and the emergence of the city-state there has been a concurring concept of justice, which he named *distributive justice,* which means that society distributes goods and resources to the citizens according to their value for society.

Of course material justice means a lot more than that. In most legislations we find expressions like reasonable, justifiable common honesty, Treu und Glauben and so forth, which are expressions of general maxims of material justice. But also the different provinces of law find guiding principles which have developed during the history of culture creating and signaling the framework of a general value-system reflecting the general conception of man and society. These general values are lying behind our legal systems and will be taken as the starting point for the legal argumentation in any particular case. They are so to speak the hermeneutic world picture which silently decides our way of arguing in social and political matters.

To these different functions of law correspond different concepts of law and different methods of legal science. Corresponding to the first aspect law is regarded as an empirical fact, politically or socially, which shall be dealt with by descriptive methods. Corresponding to the other aspect law is regarded as valid obligations, rights and duties, which must be interpreted and brought into action as guiding device for the behaviour of the population or as norm for the settlement or deciding of social conflicts. In this respect the legal science must use dogmatic methods, i.e. methods which make interpretations of authoritative texts in order to work out what rule or obligation to apply in a given situation.

Legal science may hypostatize the aspects of law and take one of the functions of law as *the* function of law and so to speak choose one model or one analogy.

In my book I mention a variety of legal theories which isolate certain aspects of law and certain functions of law and make these fundamentals of the concept of law and the legal theory.

You can only get these varieties very briefly.

Realistic Theories

The general feature of this type of legal theories is that they are conceived as empirical facts which more or less must be dealt with as such by empirical or descriptive methods.

Political theories having their starting point in the concept of state regard law as the governing device of society. *Cultural theories* on the other hand regard law more or less as a reflection of the material structure and functioning of society, a conception, which is generally accepted in ethnology and in history dealing with primitive societies. *Sociological theories* regard the legal system as a social system in cooperation with and coordinated with other social systems. Especially the Anglo-Saxon countries concentrate on the behaviour of judges, whereas the so-called system-theories of different kinds are dealing with the social behaviour or legal behaviour in different groups and the interaction between different groups in society.

Psychological theories have been found to compete with socio-logical theories especially in the U.S.A., the so-called behaviouristic theories, which regard the actions of man, like the actions of animals, as a response on an external or internal stimulus. Especially Scandinavian realism has operated with psychology as a model of law. The older representatives, particularly Hägerström and Olivecrona, regard law as a means of internalizing socially desired patterns of behaviour. This pedagogic attitude comes close to the present legal theory in the Eastern Europe, where the pedagogic element of law and politics is emphazised. For Alf Ross, the Danish legal philosopher, the psychological model is another, namely the so-called psychology of cognition, which takes its starting point in the judge's feeling of being legally obliged or the judge's legal ideology.

Ethical Theories

After World War II we have experienced a revival of natural law theories. In Germany Gustav Radbruck, in the U.S.A. Lon Fuller, in Scandinavia Frede Castberg have acted against legal positivism, which they accused of being partly responsible for the functioning of the totalitarian system during the 1930s.

Analytical Theories

Particularly Herbert Hart has in a discussion with his successor Ronald Dworkin argued that you may rather distinguish sharply between law and moral and speak about immoral law instead of illegal law or »Unrecht« as Gustav Radbruck puts it.

Hermeneutic theories in particular referred to the fact that description, also the legal description, cannot be fully objective as the language itself has built in the valuations and purposes that cause the intentional character of the language. In addition comes the recognition that the description also depends on the cultural background and the ideology behind our political and social systems. Hermeneutic theories therefore, in opposition to the analytical theories, which are mainly occupied with the analysis of the validity of law and legal system, are occupied with the problem of creating harmony between legal rule and legal fact in the process of interpretation and description in the legal decision.

Pluralis Juris

After this survey of the different functions of law in the past and present and the legal theories built upon them it must be time to return to the introductory myth about the elephant. The sages define the elephant differently because they caught hold of different parts of it and mistook that part for the whole object.

The mistake of the elephant-men, who were unable to see that they had seized only a fragment of a whole, is easy to understand if we take it for granted that they knew nothing in advance of the whole, which was an animal-organism of a certain kind. It is an experience of the Gestalt-psychology and of the hermeneutic philosophy of language as well that parts of reality are perceived and understood as parts of a whole. The hermeneutic and critical meta-science developed from these schools has emphasized the interest of cognition as constituting such fragmentary one-dimensional parts of the total perception. Finally the general relativity theory has taught us that perception both depends on and influences our measuring instruments. What has been called the hermeneutic circle is just an expression of the fact that one cannot understand the whole without knowledge of the single parts, which in their turn are understandable only as constituent parts of an organized whole. The myth implies an understanding and a criticism as well of science or philosophy. Nowadays science should be expected to be familiar with this theory of cognition, which must render it suspicious of or downright immune to the tendency found in primitive thinking to hypostatize a single aspect of the function of the whole to be the essence of things. The fundamental line of thoughts behind the above description and analysis of a number of different legal theories is just the realization that law has different functions and that legal science must consequently have different departments.

The political function of law is best studied by political and economic science, while its social and psychological function should be studied by sociology and social psychology and its cultural function by ethnology. The history of law and the comparative legal science compare the legal rules and their social functions in a vertical historical or horizontal international perspective. It is common to all these parts of legal science that they do not aim at describing and interpreting the valid or current law. Therefore their methods will in principle be descriptive, that means that they describe the law as part of working political, social, psychological and cultural systems.

Against this stands the dogmatic legal science, which being an aid of legal practice is the original and practical important part of legal science. The task of this science is the interpretation of an authoritative rule-material, the valid or current law. The dogmatic legal science describes law systematically and by means of a number of authoritative sources, and a number of methods of argumentation developed through history, which are accepted as lawful by the jurists, and which correspond with a method of argumentation applied in the legal practice. Some of these methodical features refer to normative elements (justice, fairness, equity) others to linguistic logical elements and yet others to elements of reality (teleological and pragmatic considerations).

When legal philosophers have attempted to comprise these elements under a common concept of law this has sometimes been done with reference only to the dogmatic legal science, and sometimes they have disengaged themselves from that too and treated the legal science as a social science. This latter variant has not often been lastingly successful because it has been of no outstanding interest to the customers, the legal profession. For the same reason a strictly analytical theory (pure legal theory) has been of no great success either. The debate between legal science and legal philosophy will probably go on until legal philosophy realizes and respects the fact that law has different aspects according to its different functions, and that legal science must therefore apply different methods.

The content of the legal concept in a given situation will depend on the kind of question made, which in turn depends on the specific role or function performed by the legal actor. The consulting lawyer is most interested in the probability of a certain decision of a prospective lawsuit, whereas the judge is in no need of such an external definition, but must look for an internal information of what rule he is obliged to apply. The dogmatic legal science wants to see law as a system of legal rules validly following from certain sources indicated by the principles of legal sources. Like the judges legal science is interested in the internal aspect of law not only in connection with the solution of actual problems but in order to be able to present the individual rules or solutions as parts of a systematic consistent whole. Legal sociology and social psychology are interested in the current law that means rules or behaviour which are actually complied with or which are felt to be obliging. The cognition interest of politicians is the governing effect or the oppressive character of law. Especially the latter effect, the aspect of power and sanction, must be considered to be important, while other democratic government-models attach greater importance to the public acceptance of the legal system and the individual rules. History of law, ethnology and international law for different reasons are uninterested in the aspect of sanction but want to see law as part of the national and international patterns of culture. The church and ideological movements in the widest sense conceive law as the realization of a superior order: the course of nature, the nature of man, the will of God, reason or justice (natural law), and they are unable therefore to respect the positive law unconditionally because to them its content may be invalid, in which case they have a right and a duty to resist it (right of resistance, civil disobedience).

The definition chosen is of programmatic or ideological nature connected with the underlying general conception of man and society. A command theory corresponds with an authoritarian state-concept and a collective concept of man. A sociological-functional theory of law may be the expression of a collective concept of man too, since the social utility and the distributive justice are regarded as the supreme values of society. A theory departing from the individual rights of man looks upon man as an individual and nothing else, and assigns the minimum task to society of securing the individual rights. A pluralistic legal philosophy regarding man as an individual and a social being as well recognizes that social utility and individual justice are equal, competing values and that the individual justice cannot be reduced to form part of the distributive justice. A manifestation of this fact is the increasing tendency of the legal philosophy of the latest decade of being interested in the reflective and individual oriented aspects of law at the expense of its governing and distributive functions and in turn the distributive justice which have been the main interest of the previous half century.

Private Property and Regulation

I. Development

Below I shall try to throw a sidelight on the concept of private property, its historic development and relation with the social conditions and the political organization.[1]

Private property does not exist in the outer world as particular objects or qualities of the objects. Private property is a so-called institutional fact, i.e. a plurality of elements which are organized by means of rules governed by an aim, which has its foundation in human needs and values. Therefore, we have to distinguish between the real facts, i.e. the needs and activities of human beings in relation to their surroundings, and the conceptions we form of those things.[2]

When we fully realize this distinction, we can also understand, why it is fundamentally wrong to speak of private property in a long historic perspective, and why it is at the same time meaningful. Presumably, man's fundamental need for using things in his surrounding world in order to attain the object of his desires has been relatively unchanged through all times. Like animals man has appropriated food and other things, just as individually or in groups he has limited and maintained a territory, which has yielded the material basis of his existence or the existence of the group. However, in addition to this man has been able to keep and adapt objects for tools and permanent use. For that reason human beings have had a need for creating and preserving lasting relations between themselves and outer objects and territories. Besides human beings have been able to form ideas of these relations and translate them into language, the so-called concepts.

Our ideas and consequently our concepts are formed and developed on the basis of our experiences individually as well as collectively. Therefore, they naturally have to be closely connected with the physical conditions of our life, including the prevailing socio-economic conditions at the time in question and the social organization. The ideas and concepts arise and are developed through the history of mankind. Therefore, this is naturally also true of the concept of law and the concept of right. It is a well-known fact that, some legal theorists therefore for instance deny the existence of »*objective law*«, i.e. the totality of rules of law in a given society, before this society has a formal social organization with legislature, central government and courts, whose purpose respectively are to create and administer legal rules and to settle legal disputes. Only within such organized societies exist - according to this conception - also »*subjective rights*«, i.e. »individual positions of power« secured by the rules of law. According to this conception neither law nor right exists in primitive societies or in international relations. If, on the other hand, a more functional view is adopted and interest is taken in human beings' different forms of organization and the way in which they secure the satisfaction of their needs within organized limits, it has sense to speak of law in less developed societies as well. Obviously, the former conception permits a more precise and applicable analysis of law and its structure in our time, whereas the latter makes it easier to understand the development and social function of the rules and the legal concepts. If a study of law is to be complete one therefore has to supplement these two aspects and combine a structural with a functional approach.[3]

Many things indicate that the consciousness of the individuals as well as of the human race develops from a concretizing into a generalizing perception. Children have from the beginning a very concrete perception of their surroundings, whereas the ability to make and understand generalizations and concepts develops along with growing maturity. So it also appears from analyses of the history of language that universals develop gradually on the basis of a summing up of experiences. Thus it is emphasized by the Danish classical philologist *Hartvig Frisch* in his book on power and law in antiquity[4] that the abstraction »good« does not occur in the Greek language until in the 6th century at the earliest. Before this time the concept occurs in a functional or instrumental sense as »good at« something.[5]

»*Good*« (↔ evil) as an abstraction develops on the basis of the practical experiences of many generations. So it is also assumed by the two prominent legal historians, *Max Kaser* and *H. J. Wolff*[6] that the concept of right as idea has arisen as a number of conflicts between individuals and groups has been settled in a certain way, which eventually develops into an established practice gradually making people expect a similar conflict to be settled in the same way. As such expectations gain ground, they separate from the concrete conflicts and result in the creation of the abstraction »right«. Thus, historically it is a right of petition (writ), which gives rise to creation of the abstraction »right«, and later on the acceptance of the existence of an individual right gives ground for the putting forward of a legal petition. As late as the classical Roman law they have not detached themselves from the starting point, as it is the legal petition (actio), which constitutes the subjective right. A corresponding situation is found within English mediaeval law (writ).

If we turn to the Nordic provincial laws from the 12th and the 13th centuries, we can observe, how corresponding legal actions are dependent on the existence of a special access to complaint, which is left to private initiative. As in the original Roman law the case is a private matter between two individuals, who put the conflict in the hands of a mediator or an arbitrator chosen jointly by the parties. It is a generally accepted view among legal sociologists and legal ethnologists that the embryo of an organized solution of conflicts must be sought for in such an institution of mediation and arbitration, which is replaced by actual organized courts concurrently with the formation of a central political power. In the old Greek city-states and in the Nordic peasant communities it was originally the people's assemblies, which convened and settled the conflicts in an attempt to maintain peace in the communities.[7]

It is obvious that at any rate the Roman jurists have had rather unambiguous ideas of private rights, among these also of a special property right consisting in a person's special dominion over a thing (dominium), and an obligation consisting in a bond between two persons (nexum, obligatio). Only a much later posterity has in these ideas interpreted complete property rights and obligations in the form of a 'ius in re' and a 'ius ad rem'. No more than the Roman legal conception recognized any fundamental distinction between ius in re and ius ad rem and any fundamental distinction between procedural law and material law existed any distinction between private law and public law. All in all the concepts and contents of ownership could be said to be identical with the possibilities that the system of procedure implied to the person who claimed to have dominion over a thing. In Roman law as well as in the early mediaeval societies the execution of the judicial decision was left to private enforcement.

Concurrently with the development of the medieaval feudal societies there is a change of the conception of ownership in real property, which is presumed to belong to the king or on the Continent to the emperor. The king or the emperor enfeoffs his vasals with larger or smaller territories, which are then given to the peasants as tenancy. However, it would be incorrect to describe such feudal rights of use as rights of private or public law in land in a modern sense.

The later European natural law is the first to make fully developed ideas of subjective rights as a concept.[8] The European natural law originates in the Catholic moral philosophy. However, in accordance with the classical tradition the Catholic moral philosophy operates with the concept of the »law of nature« (lex naturæ), whereas the Protestant so-called rationalist natural law of the 17th and the 18th centuries operates with the concept of »natural right« *(ius naturæ)*. This reflects the development, which has taken place in the experience of man's situation from the 13th to the 17th centuries. In the meantime we have the great discoveries and the economic development especially within urban trade, which lays the groundwork for the Renaissance and individualism, and consequently for the idea that each individual has special natural rights.

The conceptions of state and law in the Middle Ages were based on the presumption that God's law, which is eternal and unchangeable, together with customary law is prescriptive to human life, whereas the secular princes have the task of maintaining peace and order in the name of God. During the Renaissance the conception arose that there is a human legislative power, a sovereignty, which is originally believed to lie with the secular prince. By this the groundwork for the conflict between emperor and pope was laid, in which among others *Dante* - as we already know - opposed the pope. - This idea had its consistent form in Machiavelli and in the later European absolute monarchies, where the sovereignty lay with the king (the State that's I!).

While the theorists of the Renaissance assumed that the sovereignty, i.e. the legislative power, lay with the prince, it was assumed by *Hugo Grotius* and his imitators in the 17th century that the sovereignty lay with each individual. From this the conclusion was drawn that law-making in any form therefore has to seek its grounds in each individual's own rational will. The laws of the society had to be based on a so-called social contract consisting in the individuals' presupposed approval of the social institution. Only through this it was possible to justify the intervention in the freedom of the individuals which the laws and the enforcement of the laws implied.

It was a natural consequence of this starting point that the creation of rights according to private law was conceived as the individuals' own self-legislation, and for that reason it was just as unlimited as the legislation according to the social contract. A consequence of this was the adoption of a general freedom of agreement, which was a disengagement from the traditional types of contracts within Roman law.

The English philosopher *John Locke* considers - as mentioned below - private property as a natural right on the same lines as human rights and legislative authority. Everybody is entitled to the profit of the work that he has performed. - Therefore, »Danske Lov« (1683) V.1.1. prescribes that everybody is bound by his oral as well as by his written promises. By the promise some of the liberty of the promisor is transferred to the promisee, who then by virtue of a special moral power has a right (ius) over the promisor. This primary right based on the promise is supplemented by a secondary right of the promisee to use force against the promisor. This force is considered to be based on the social contract, which legitimates the power of the state.

Private property is also believed originally to be based on such an access to make a claim against another person, but in accordance with a traditional conception private property is considered to be justified by a special dominion *(dominium)* over a thing. However, this dominion automatically implies obligations to everybody and a right of the owner to make a claim against the person, who interferes in his property rights. But consequently any right is taken to involve an obligation for one person or an indefinite number of persons.

It is self-evident that such a conception of law reflects the interest of the growing middle classes. Concurrently with the economic development of the urban trade a political self-consciousness arose and there was a desire for having a share in the social influence. Referring to the sovereignty of the people the French Revolution in 1789 and the later bourgeois revolutions during the 19th century were carried through.

As the revolutionary philosophy deriving from natural law drained away in bourgeois democracies there was a need for legitimating the creation of law of the new society independently of each individual's will. Therefore, the 19th century is everywhere characterized by an extensive legal positivism, which conceives objective law as the orders of the sovereign, i.e. the state. As early as the end of the 18th century *Immanuel Kant* had separated law from moral and in doing so founded the legal positivism. The German legal theorist *von Savigny* saw to the further development of these ideas; in continuation of Kant's liberal theory of the state he wanted to keep private law out of the sovereignty of the state. Consequently Savigny introduced a fundamental distinction between public law, which was considered to be based on the will of the state, and private law, which was considered to be based on the will of the individuals. The object of the state is only to create the outer framework and a system of compulsion for the realization of the private social life, the so-called »watchmanstate«.[9]

Another consequence of this is that it is possible to define the private subjective rights as a power of will, a power founded on the private will, but secured by objective law. By the distinction between private law and public law Savigny has introduced a distinction which makes it difficult conceptually to justify social limitations of private property. However, by principally recognizing legal positivism a door has been opened to a recognition in principle of any social limitation of the private property, which is in accordance with the constitution in force at the time in question.

This was the consequence that the Danish jurist *A. S. Ørsted* draw from this theory at the beginning of the 19th century. As a prominent official and politician A. S. Ørsted influenced the Danish legislation during the first half of the 19th century.[10]

The English philosopher *Jeremy Bentham* rejects the existence of subjective rights, which he conceives only as fictive manifestations of the sovereign's orders through the objective law; also within German theory it is assumed that rights do not exist - they are nothing but mere forms of thoughts that make possible a survey and control of complicated sets of rules of law. This is the conception of law that we shall meet in the modern so-called realist theories of law.

However, at the end of the last century it became still more evident that objective law as well as subjective rights are not mere conceptual constructions or public or private expressions of will. It is recognized that the law is a means of achieving human objects which again derive from fundamental human interests. As objective law is the result of a struggle between political forces, subjective rights become a legally protected interest. By this it has been recognized in principle that objective law and subjective rights are political results of socially effective interests.

Although the European constitutions contain provisions which recognize the inviolability of private property, it is recognized, however, in § 73 of the present Danish Constitution that private property must yield to the public interest. - Private property must be given up or tolerate restrictions when it is required out of consideration for the public good, but only in return of full compensation. However, at the same time it is recognized that private property is not unlimited. Private property must not be exercised spitefully, and concurrently with the growth of the society and the social development during the 20th century it has been recognized to an increased extent that private persons must endure general limitations of private property in so far as it is necessary for the social planning and the social welfare. On the other hand, such general limitations of private property do not involve any claim to compensation. An important problem is, however, to limit the general restrictions of private property, which do not admit the owner to compensation, from expropriations, which incur an obligation to pay compensation in full to the owner.

The so-called realistic theories of law have all by virtue of a fundamental positivism of law left this decision to the legislature, which is said to give a more precise definition and delimitation of private property in its laws. Private property is - as expressed by the Danish legal theorist *Alf Ross* - nothing but a terminological auxiliary concept connecting a set of legal facts with the legal effects provided by the laws.[11] Characteristically, therefore, in his handbook of constitutional law Alf Ross goes very far in the direction of assuming that in principle the legislature can pass any limitation whatsoever of private property.

It is not possible here to amplify the legal philosophical debate on the concept of right. As already mentioned some theories will completely empty the concept of right of any content and make it a linguistic designation of objective law concerning the relationship between persons and objects. Others consider subjective rights as mere reflexes of the system of procedure. However, it is common to these conceptions that »right« and »private property« have no independent content.

Another Nordic tradition dating back to the end of the last century does not empty the concept of right and especially the concept of private property of all content, even though it breaks up private property into several legal relations and several actual and legal rights of the owner.[12] According to this conception private property contains four rights: 1) the right to an actual use of the object in so far as it does not conflict with limitations, if any, provided by the law, 2) the right to legal disposal of the object, 3) the right to use the object as a security when raising loans, and 4) the right to pass on the object.

I shall not here make a detailed evaluation of the different conceptions of the concept of right. I only want to point out that in my opinion one ought to be wary of defining objective law as well as subjective rights as monistic concepts.

It is beyond doubt that the concept of right is attached to important human functions and interests, as it appears from history. This is a fact that one has to take into consideration when discussing the concept of right in a legal political sense. If the concept of right is to be discussed in a legal dogmatic sense, it will on the other hand be more natural to use the so-called realistic concept of right, which conceives the rights as an abbreviated expression of the rules embodied in objective law.

However, it can not be ignored that the choice of concept of right has an ideological aspect, which in case of doubt can determine the argumentation. To a Liberal conception the freedom of action is fundamental, so limitations of this must have a specific legitimation; therefore, it is natural here to conceive private property (and the other private rights) as something more than the total of the rules of objective law. Private property (and other rights) has according to this conception specific contents which secure the legitimate freedom of action in relation to an object to such an extent that it does not conflict with the limits, if any, put on it in positive law, i.e. a constitutional right. On the other hand, a Socialist conception, which does not primarily let the individual freedom of action come before other considerations, will to a higher degree be inclined to conceive the rights as mere reflexes of objective law, i.e. a »social function«.

II. Perspectives

We have seen, how the concept of »property« has developed through the ages, and how it has got its complete expression at a certain time in a given political, economic and ideological environment.

The concept is systematically connected with the general conceptions of the anthropology and society of man, which (i.e. conceptions) have arisen partly by virtue of, partly in opposition to a historical development. The society can be conceived as a collective whole, of which each individual is part-elements, and as an association of *individuals*. In the former respect the conception is collectivistic, in the latter respect it is individualistic.

It appears from the historical introduction that primitive societies founded on subsistence economy are organized on the basis of a collectivistic human conception. Here the family is the principal element in the structure of society. Legally it is the family, who has rights and is liable in legal matters; especially, the family is responsible for breaches of law, as it also has a right to enforce the law o. reaction. The contract does not play a decisive part, as the status relations guarantee each individual his share of the total economic profits. As a consequence of this fact the right of private property is not of great importance. In the nomadic society the flock belongs to the family, and in the agrarian society of the Middle Ages the land belongs in principle to the king, whereas the right of use is passed on through the families.

It is not until the dissolution of the status relations and the introduction of the division of labour within commerce, shipping, and trade in the urban society that the individuals are conceived as the foundation of the society. Consequently each individual becomes personally responsible for his actions, and he is able to enter into personal obligations by agreement. Money emerges as a means of payment, as at the same time there are a need for and a faculty of making abstract ideas symbolizing private person's power over and interest in the result of his work.

Property is fully developed as a concept in the 17th and the 18th centuries, and at the same time economic growth opens up the possibility of an advanced urban economy.

Particularly, the Englishman *John Locke* (1632-1704) emphasized the connection of private property with human rights. In his opinion a natural consequence of the freedom of the individual was that he was entitled to the result of the work that he himself had performed. This connection between freedom and property is already expressed in *Hugo Grotius'* (1583-1645) natural law. According to this the individual's freedom of action is conceived as a right, of which he may dispose

116

and which he may surrender to others by virtue of the individual's power based on his rational will to enter into obligations by agreements and by the laws.

These conceptions of society and property based on humans' being free and equal individuals underlay the bourgeois opposition of the Enlightenment against the despotic state, which had replaced the feudal society of the Middle Ages. These conceptions of human beings and society are expressed in the American Constitution of 1776 and the French Declaration of Rights of Man from 1789. Instead of »liberty, equality, and fraternity« it is, however, »liberty, equality, and private property«. It is this conception of society gravitating towards Liberalism that becomes predominant in Europe during the 19th century, in Denmark with the Constitution of 1849.

It is important to the citizens to emphasize their freedom from compulsion of the state and the corresponding freedom to use their faculties and possibilities of making the greatest possible economic profits, The philosophical basis was found in Kant's (1724-1804) social philosophy, which took as its starting point the freedom of individuals, which should be the foundation of the state and consequently of right and morality. Considering other people's equal right to freedom the individual is completely free to arrange his life and act on his wishes. The object of the state should only be to maintain order internally and peace externally and altogether to avoid to interfere with the citizens' private dealings, the so-called »watchmanstate«.

Inspiration could be sought in the English »utilitarism« as well. *Jeremy Bentham* (1748-1832) found that the morality had to be in proper relation to the use of the act, i.e. the happiness that it caused, and that the object of the society therefore was to ensure the greatest happiness of the greatest number. *Adam Smith* (Wealth of Nations 1776) founded the economic liberalism in opposition to the mercantilistic economic theory of despotism, which the state considered to be represented in the national product. However, Adam Smith assumed that - without interference of the state and in competition with others - the individual's own striving to make his own profits as good as possible tended towards the greatest possible advantage of the society.

It is evident that the condition of this »bourgeois equilibrium state« is that the human beings actually are equally well-developed to make the most of the existing possibilities. The conception of private property as a complete freedom to take possession of the profits of one's work and to dispose of real property or movable property acquired without violating others' equal right implies an economy which is essentially based on trade and commerce actually placing the actors in the same strategic positions.

It is evident that this is a philosophy suitable for a small élite who has been sufficiently educated to take part in the public debate, which is the ideological basis of democracy, and who has sufficient means to utilize the economic possibilities. The formal nature of human rights is emphasized by *Anatole Frances* in his well-known ironic maxim: It is forbidden all Frenchmen to sleep under the bridges of the Seine, to beg in the streets and to steal bread.

However, it is beyond doubt that economic liberalism and private property were very important for the economic growth and consequently for the increased prosperity at the end of the 18th century. By this the groundwork was laid for the very process of industrialization, especially in Great Britain and France, which again resulted in a complete change of the practical and the ideological basis of the society. The fact is that industrialization caused an increased need for capital and a need for larger markets, in order to be able to start a mass production and make it profitable. The need for capital was ensured through the creation of banks and companies which introduced abstract relations between property, management and responsibility. Concurrently the personal relations between employer and employee - which formerly existed within trade - was dissolved and replaced by impersonal relations. This meant that the wage-earner had to sell his working power in the factories in competition with others without security for a subsistence level. The increased need for markets resulted in an international competition for colonies and raw materials.

As early as the middle of the 19th century *Karl Marx* (1818-1883) had analysed the mechanism of capitalism and its consequences for the economy and the development of society.[13] He was aware of the fact that private property played another part in an industrialized society; the anonymous relations between Capital and Labour resulted in an increasing impoverishment of the new working classes and in a still growing concentration of capital, as Capital breeds capital. »The surplus value« of the work (i.e. the difference between the result of the work and the wages) is accumulated as »profit«. Therefore, Marx prophesied that as a necessity society developed into a Socialist and later into a Communist society, where the workers have jointly taken over the property of the means of production. However, at the same time he and his like-minded persons worked actively for the promotion of these political ends.

In this century it has appeared, however, that the revolution has not taken place, where it - according to Marx - ought to take place: in the highly developed industrial societies of Western Europe, but on the contrary where it ought not to take place: in Eastern Europe and in the developing countries. There are several reasons for this but first of all the fundamental circumstance that it has been possible to change society by means of rules of law and agreements. Marx himself believed that the rules of law were part of the »ideological superstructure« derived from the »material foundation« of society, which in his opinion was decisive for the historical development. Therefore, he did not believe that the development could be changed and controlled by means of rules of law. For that reason he was convinced that the rules of law would »wither« together with the state in the future Communist society, where the contradiction between »private« and »public« interests would disappear along with private property.

Experience has proved the opposite and by this in fact denied the »scientific« basis of Marxism. On the contrary it has turned out that by means of a comprehensive legislation and collective agreements on the labour market it has been possible to carry through: 1) a division of the profits of the process of production between Capital and Labour, 2) a redistribution among the citizens in general by means of taxes, rates, and dues, and 3) an extensive social, health and culture legislation, which has completely removed the direct connection between the individual efforts and the final economic profits.

In actual fact the building up of the modern Welfare State started (in Denmark) during World War I, when the State intervened in the economic life by a number of measures to secure production and distribution of goods and services. All over the world private economy became dependent on the state's financing and control of the war industry, the supplies of foodstuffs, and the need for transportation. When in the 1920s attempts were made to withdraw the engagement of the state in private economy, it was a contributory cause to the international crisis, which was brought under control together with the recognition of *Keynes'* general economic theory. This theory presupposed a permanent state responsibility for national economics and therefore also for the private economic sector.

The same social political interests resulted in a similar regulation of the agricultural policy. Regard for self-sufficiency and fight against unemployment led to a restrictive agricultural legislation, which made unrestrained parcelling out and amalgamations of farm land illegal. As early as the 18th century the maintenance of optimum undivided holdings had been favoured by means of rules of succession. At the same time a law concerning the preservation of forests was introduced in order to ensure the supply of sufficient ship timbers. And by the Barring and Entail Act of 1916 and the later agricultural legislation it was tried to counteract the amalgamation of landed estates; instead the object was to further the breaking up of estates into smaller holdings. During recent years the economic and technological development has resulted in an opposite movement, which furthers the creation of larger production units. However, the agricultural sector has been thoroughly regulated along with the establishment of the new international market organizations (the Common Market a.o.) as part of a common European agrarian policy. To this must be added the general and special rules of depreciation.

The »Kanslergade-compromise« at the beginning of the 1930s was the first step towards this welfare policy in Denmark. In principle it recognized the obligation of society to preserve agricultural industry as well as urban trade and combine them with a social policy ensuring a minimum of social welfare and in this way also a sufficient demand to keep the economy going. The price of this was naturally increasing taxes as part of a social distribution policy and a fiscal policy with the express purpose of counteracting the strongest fluctuations of the market. Society took over the responsibility for education, pensioning, health insurance and health services, matters concerning communication and roads, supply of energy, and in the post-war era to an increasing extent child-minding and cultural life.

Thus, in recent times there is no limit to the tasks of society in fields, which were earlier considered to be subject to private initiative and responsibility. Consequently there was an acute economic schism between *internal* and *external* costs. When society takes over the costs of education and sickness, of communication and roads and so on, these costs become external costs; i.e. costs that do not enter into the private economic calculation, but are considered as free goods. What from a private economic point of view seems to be a good piece of business may from a social economic point of view be a bad piece of business. As an example of this is often mentioned the relation between private and collective traffic, in as much as the roads can be used free of charge by private persons, whereas trade has to pay for public transportation.

In recent times a number of welfare political, health political and social political factors have been included in the regulation of trade. At the same time it has been required that trade must obtain the permission of the authorities to build and carry on their business according to the rules in the town and planning legislation, the factory and health legislation. The purpose here is to make the most of the resources invested by the state in the development of towns, in schools and social institutions, and roads, etc. Further objects as to the health and welfare of the population are combined with regard for a reduction of the expenses for injury and medical treatment and lost earnings.

However, the interests of society in securing the citizens' welfare go still further. By means of an extensive fiscal legislation it is endeavoured to direct production and employment indirectly, at the same time as quantitative restrictions in foreign trade are replaced by customs rules. Firstly, these rules favour the division of labour within large international markets, e.g. the E.E.C., secondly, at global level attempts are made to promote an international competition and di-

120

vision of labour; but it is endeavoured as well to protect the trade of your own country against unreasonable competition from developing countries with low costs. However, also at international level there are attempts at an intentional governing of national and international economies by means of agreements, at one time regulating and liberating trade by making possible competition on equal terms.

We have seen, how a bourgeois Liberal democracy implies a society of free and equal individuals, who in dialogue and competition with one another promote their own interests with the presumed consequence that it would tend towards the greatest possible benefit to the public, i.e. to society. Thus, ideologically democracy involves a pluralistic society, where the freedom of action can actually be used for choosing between several possibilities. The economic tool of this form of organization is private property, which is supposed to consist in a special tie between a person and his thing and a special »freedom-of-action-sphere« about this relation between person and thing. On the other hand, there is a necessary connection between freedom and responsibility, as the private person is supposed to be able to appropriate the profit of his own labour, whereas the values created by the society do not in the same way »naturally« go to private persons.

We have seen that to an increasing extent society is participating in and has taken a considerable general responsibility for the national and the international economy. Thus, it stands to reason that trade cannot claim in the same way as earlier to be responsible for its operations, and nowadays no one within trade would dream of wishing the state out of economics; already the crisis of the 1920s showed that there was no going back to the »watchmanstate« of the past, and in our time the public sector is of vital importance to economics. In addition to this there is the market policy.

To this must be added - as already mentioned - all the »external« costs, which society has taken over from and pays for trade. And as a new thing in our time must finally be added: various (public) subsidies; originally it was especially agriculture which in the 1930s gave up its »liberal« foundation and by this the maxim: »Let go down, what is not payable!« However, nowadays not only agriculture is subsidized - before the E.E.C.-membership it was national subsidies and afterwards E.E.C.-subsidies - but also shipbuilding industry and house building have obtained special guarantees of the rate of interest and subsidies. And subsidies to trade and regional development have provided capital for works and productions, which had not otherwise been carried into effect.

In so far as society takes over »the costs« of production it is completely in accordance with the ideology of Liberalism that society must assume an increasing part of the responsibility for and thus the influence on trade. At the same time a concentration has - as indicated - taken place at a national as well as at an international level. This development has resulted in an abolition or a weakening of the competition, which is the ideological counterpart to freedom and responsibility, and of the factor, which justifies freedom, as it is presumed to protect the interests of *the public*. For the fact is that it has never been overlooked that democracy must safeguard the interests of the public; otherwise it will become addicted to egoism, dictatorship of the majority or dictatorship of the minority.

Therefore, you ought to be aware of the fact that a real *pluralism* in trade ensuring an actually free choice is an economic condition of a political democracy. Monopolies and international companies endeavouring to abolish competition by means of amalgamations and agreements are probably better fit for developing the national and international markets and for making resources. However, on the other hand they are able to ignore - by restraints of trade - the interests of the public and the effective development of the resources on a long view to the benefit of society.

At national level attempts have been made to counteract this risk by monopoly control and prohibition of establishment of cartels; at international level it has been argued in favour of the international organizations as a sufficiently strong »defence« against the multinational companies. However, in both cases increasing national and international bureaucracies are required in order to establish a sufficiently strong and expert counteraction to the national and international companies, which have an interest in and can afford the financing of the necessary expertise and which benefit by »having the lead« as far as plans and strategy are concerned.

Here we face one of the greatest problems of our democratic form of life. Our political systems are based on the condition that the population as a rule elects its representatives by a secret vote every four years. Until the next election these representatives are to safeguard their electors' interests and administer their »sovereignty« by passing the necessary acts. The modern technological welfare society has made a considerable instability in the conditions of life, which form the intellectual basis of democracy.

The time horizon has been widened. In the earlier relatively static society it was reasonable to assume that electoral periods of four years were convenient intervals. Nowadays, however, trade has to plan on a much longer view owing to the depreciation of the heavy costs for development and investment necessitated by the modern form of production. Therefore, private economic life needs the best and consequently the highest paid experts, who in return plan on a qualified basis the future production including the development of new technology.

On the other hand the political system calls for shortsighted decisions, i.e. within the frames of the next electoral period of four years. Thus, it is evident that the politicians are subject to a constant pressure by the immediate, urgent problems and by the population's wishes to get the unpleasant effects abolished at the shortest possible notice. This pressure may result in the fact that the politicians are fixed on single-problems without getting the opportunity to recognize and draw attention to coherence and the long-term timeframe for balancing unpleasant conditions and advantages. For instance, it may be a temptation to raise loans abroad to finance a deficit on the balance of payment instead of lowering the effective income during a depression, although the future consequences may be extremely unpleasant.

Altogether democracy may tend towards a service democracy granting the population what it thinks it needs of services, which in relation to the individuals are »private«, as they benefit from them in the form of free services, whereas, on the other hand, retrenchments are »public« in the sense that their only effect is an abstract tax relief, unless they affect a field, in which the individual has a »private« interest. Therefore, public retrenchments are always met with general approval, until the concrete retrenchments are allotted. The well-earned rights of the recipients as well as the occupational interests of the staff organizations will as a rule be able to stop effective retrenchments on the budget; but they will in return be able to subject the politicians to strong pressure in favour of an increase in the standard.

Another example is the energy debate, where rises in the price of oil and the supply situation seem to speak clearly in favour of a fast development of nuclear technology in Denmark, as there will be an increasing demand for energy in the future. Even though no objective facts indicate that nuclear power involves greater risks than other energy forms a (organized) public feeling has so far thrown obstacles in the way of a political decision. Thus, a lot of things speak in favour of the assumption that the risk or the waste problem is not the real motive for the organized opposition to nuclear power; it is rather a political exploitation of a public fear of modern technology and its consequences for the social and economic life and effects on the welfare of the citizens.

And now the wheel has come full circle in a way. The economic life has to plan far ahead and in doing so it has to take into consideration the existing technology or the technology to come, because human beings probably cannot help utilizing their possibilities. On the other hand, the democratic system cannot within its time limits invest in long-term planning. Therefore, the economic life has had a relatively free scope to plan for society. The industrial development began during the last century, and railway lines were built regardless of physical and social environments, which were highly changed by pollution in the widest sense. Concurrently with this development the town population was proletarianized partly by ruined workmen partly by inmigrated farm workers. However, all this took place in accordance with the prevailing political ideology at that time, which was the »watchmanstate«.

By this it has at one time been indicated that this development had not been tolerated under the political circumstances of our time, which of course is a completely unrealistic assumption, but on the other hand this development laid the groundwork for the Welfare State in our time. Nowadays, however, the development within technology has also resulted in great social changes in spite of the fact that the political ideology has been changed in favour of a politically guided society. - I only have to remind you of the social revolution that private motoring caused especially in the post-war era. Without the car the development of »family houses« outside the towns had been impossible, and therefore also the development (systematically connected with the above mentioned) of the shopping system with supermarkets and discount stores.

On the other hand, we have seen, how the building of such shopping centres do not only influence the structure of trade and industry, but also the need for traffic systems and town planning development. For example the town planning development of the Århus-area was broken up by the establishment of such a centre at a time, when the area was administered by a plurality of local councils competing for tax means and facilities and thrusting on to the neighbouring councils the costs for investments in roads, etc.

These examples are sufficient for the illustration of the present scepticism towards and distrust of trade, which used not to cover the »external« costs (nor has it ever had to do so, - at that time it did nothing but what the population wanted it to do). The prospect of the fact that the EDP-technology and the electronic technology as a whole tend towards a promotion of larger units has given rise to a general fear of the consequences of this development. The division of labour has become still more pronounced, and the individual processes consist to an increasing extent in controlling. Thus, the connection between your own efforts and the finished product and its sale and application becomes still more abstract and consequently incomprehensible. In the same way the political connections between the state and social services and between the different elements in politics become completely incomprehensible to ordinary people.

This has resulted in an increasing flood of »people's movements« or »grassroot-movements«, especially against a concrete case, like for instance the E.E.C., nuclear power, or pollution. The ideological value adduced in support of these movements is as a rule the request for »participation in decision-making« or »participant democracy«, which means that political decisions are to be made by persons affected by these. Ostensibly these movements are necessary and reasonable tendencies in a democratic process of development tending towards the greatest possible self-determination and liberty of choise. But in actual fact they are a denial of the representativity which is the condition of democracy's serving the public rather than personal or local interests; especially there is a risk that the weak and uneducated will be exploited by the well-educated (»the terror of the loudvoiced«). Also the irrational rejection of expert knowledge and facts is alarming for a rational creation of opinion, which is the condition of an actual democratic decision-making process and not a dictatorship of the majority.

Here the mass media - especially the electronic ones - come to play an important part together with elementary human and therefore also political conditions. The mass media go in for contrete, dramatic, and exotic things, because human beings in general think concretely and to an increasing extent have difficulties about complicated economic and political relations. This results in the fact that the representation of real life becomes still more kaleidoscopic and incomprehensible; besides the media can to a still higher degree be used for a manipulation of the public opinion by making pseudo-events and by arranging events as pseudo-events. The politicians, who have to play on the conditions of the media, get far away from the fundamental ideal of democracy: the qualified debate among sensible people.

Thus, we face several dilemmas. To an increasing extent trade has to tolerate that its basis of decision has been assumed by public bureaucracies, which are to evaluate the concrete projects in relation to labour, environment, town development, and health legislation and sometimes the profitableness. This is the price of society's participating in and sharing the responsibility for private economy. On the other hand it is trade that has to plan far ahead, as the democratic system cannot operate with a longer timeframe than the electoral period. The various people's movements are symptoms of this dilemma.

Democracy is based on a real pluralism in trade; but on the other hand democracy has difficulty in securing that the control of trade does not fall to the ground, so that trade plans the development of society and not the other way round.

The question is then if democracy in a traditional sense is possible in the future at all, or if an authoritative rule, i.e. Socialist or Corporate, is necessary to prevent the development of society from falling apart in chaos. The question is also how far in actual fact we have already got in this direction in the East and in the West.

In the people's democracies of the East private property of the means of production has formally been abolished, as the public bureaucracies under the leadership of the commissars of the Party plan production and sale from a political evaluation of what are the real »needs« of the citizens. However, marketing problems demonstrate that articles, quality, and price are not always in accordance with the real »wants« of the population. A Polish economist said some years ago to the Danish television that a centralistic and bureaucratic economy was suitable only during war, revolution and during the building up of a modern production potential. Afterwards nothing but the market mechanism will be able to guarantee an effective exploitation of the resources and a current adjustment to the still more refined demand for goods and services.

It is evident that on the other hand a centralistic and bureaucratic economy is fitted for planning far ahead and for ensuring in the first place the carrying into effect of political objects, and secondly the consideration for essential changes in the factors forming part of the economy, such as the energy. The East European countries can very quickly extend a series of atomic power plants without having to consider the public feeling.

Several Western democracies have already taken the consequences of these circumstances and have established an actual »corporate« bureaucracy consisting of the trade organizations - especially employers' associations and trade union congresses - and a state and local bureaucracy administering the political process of guidance and appropriation. In Sweden they have gone still further, as the State has supported not only trade, but also to a large extent has bought unprofitable parts of the heavy industries, among other things mines and shipbuilding yards, in order to maintain employment. In Norway the politicians have had a decisive influence on the financing, as the State has taken over the majority of seats in the managements of the banks. In Denmark we have so far only indirectly supported certain parts of trade; this fact is due - among other things - to the structure of our trade, which consists of a lot of small works in contrast to few and large key industries.

Trade in Denmark has therefore in principle refused to receive general State aid, realizing the connection between freedom, responsibility and influence. Consequently, it has also rejected the idea of the Danish Trade Union Congress concerning a general system of economic democracy, which was to be based on a central fund consisting of contributions from a general turnover tax. On the other hand, Danish trade has recognized the idea of a spread of private property of the means of production by voluntary sale of shares and profit-sharing.

It is hard to see, how to make the wage-earners and especially their organizations restrain their wage claims, without knowing for certain that the advantage of this is not capitalized by the factory owners. On the other hand, the competitive power of Danish trade will be seriously threatened, if the inflationary development is not checked, and the raising of loans abroad is not brought to an end. But there is doubtlessly no political majority in favour of such a legislation, which, however, would not contravene § 73 of the Danish Constitution, no more than the Norwegian Bank Act. And if it is true that there is a connection between economic pluralism and representative democracy, it is not recommendable from a democratic point of view, as the financing as well as the production affect the decisions, which are utilized in market economic processes.

This third dilemma between market economy and democracy on the one hand and the demands for the financing of trade by means of central funds on the other is perhaps our greatest political problem. It is difficult to see how to solve the problem. However, there is after all still reason for scepticism on a short view; but on the other hand there is reason for some optimism believing in human beings' practical interests and a sensible process of adaptation on a long view.

Notes

1) A more extensive sketch of the historical evolution is made in my article: Der Begriff des Eigentums in geschichtlicher und gegenwärtiger Betrachtung im Bereich der öffentlichen Planung, in: Festschrift für Helmut Schelsky, 1978, p. 249. About theories of legal concepts in general, see *Alf Ross*, Virkelighed og Gyldighed i Retslæren, 1934, Kap. VIII-XII, p. 168 ff.; *Karl Olivecrona*, Law as Fact, 2. ed., 1971, Ch. 6, p. 135 ff.; *R. Dubischar*, Grundbegriffe des Rechts, 1968, Kap. 4, p. 30 ff.; about concepts in general, see *Stig Jørgensen*, Typologie und »Realismus« in der neueren Rechtswissenschaft, 1971; see also *Stig Jørgensen*, Law and Society, 1971, p. 8 ff.; *Stig Jørgensen*, Vertrag und Recht, 1968, p. 49 ff.

2) See *Stig Jørgensen*, Idealism and Realism in Jurisprudence, Scandinavian Studies in Law, vol. 21, 1977, p. 95.

3) See *Stig Jørgensen*, Law and Society l.c. (note 1) Ch. I.

4) *Hartvig Frisch*, Magt og Ret i Oldtiden, 1944, p. 278 ff.

5) See *Stig Jørgensen*, Symmetry and Justice, in. Values in Law, 1978, p. 59.; *Stig Jørgensen*, Legal Positivism and Natural Law l.c., p. 103 ff.

6) *Max Kaser*, Das altrömische Ius, 1949, and Lex und Ius civile, Landesreferate z. VIII. Intern. Kongress für Rechtsvergleichung, ed. by E. v. Caemmerer and Konrad Zweigert, 1967, p. 3 ff.; *H. J. Wolff*, Debt and Assumpsit in the Light of Comparative Legal History, in: Irish Jurist, 1966, p. 316 ff.; *C. W. Westrup*, Rettens opståen, 1940, p. 36 ff.

7) *Torstein Eckhoff*, The Mediator, the Judge and the Administrator in Conflict Resolution, in: Acta Sociologica, 1966, p. 36 ff.; *Stig Jørgensen*, Symmetry l.c. (note 5) p. 65 ff., and Legal Positivism l.c. (note 5) p. 114 ff.

8) See to the following, *Stig Jørgensen*, Legal Positivism l.c. (note 5) p. 117 f., and *Stig Jørgensen*, Vertrag und Recht, 1968, p. 141 ff., and *Karl Olivecrona*, Law as Fact l.c. (note 1) p. 142 ff.

9) *Gerhard Dilcher*, Der rechtswissenschaftliche Positivismus, wissenschaftliche Methode, Sozialphilosophie, Gesellschaftspolitik, in: Archiv für Rechts- und Sozialphilosophie, 1975, p. 497 ff.

10) *Stig Jørgensen*, Grundzüge der Entwicklung der skandinavischen Rechtswissenschaft, in: Juristenzeitung, 1970, p. 529 ff.; and in: Legal Philosophical Library, ed. by Enrico Pattaro, 1980, p. 25 ff.

11) *Stig Jørgensen*, On Law and Justice, 1974, p. 177 ff.

12) *Fr. Vinding Kruse*, Das Eigentumsrecht, 1931, p. 156 ff.

13) *Stig Jørgensen*, Values in Law l.c. (note 5) p. 18 ff.

Contract as a Social Form of Life

It is a good idea to bring Japanese and European lawyers together to present their views on the general conception and use of contract in their respective countries in order to improve the understanding of the common features of the means of exchanging goods and other values in the different cultures, but also to realize why there are - and must be - differences in the way we handle and describe what we are actually doing. Professor Kitagawa mentioned in his paper the general comparative law principle that different cultures facing the same practical problems solve them in the same way but use their special traditions, concepts and institutions to reach the solution.

In his paper Professor Kitagawa has put emphasis on the special devices Japanese business law in modern times has developed to protect the consumers against unfair conditions in general form contracts. Due to the special political tradition in Japan that job has been done by administrative and not by legislative and judicial means. In my paper I will try to give a general view of the instrument and concept of contract throughout the history of man, but I hope that my exposé will also throw a sidelight on the interesting development in modern Japanese law.

In the previous century the famous English legal historian John Summer Maine coined the phrase: From status to contract. In an earlier book (Vertrag und Recht, 1968) with reference to the growing use of standard form contracts I changed the phrase into: From status to contract and back again. What I am hinting at, which I shall mention in my paper, is that Japanese contract law so to speak jumped into the modern technological world one hundred years ago, when the golden age of contract was already declining. Mass production demanded mass sales at standardized conditions designed by the manufacturers without special bargaining with the individual customer. That, of course, affected the content and use of contract which to a substantial extent became a »take it or leave it«. In labour law the growing trade unions protected the interests of the upcoming working class in general agreements with the employers' organizations. But in the other departments of contract law there were no strong interest groups to protect the interests of the general population which was often overlooked by the industries which protected their mutual interests in negotiated agreed documents, which met the demand for new law where the legislation could not keep up with the evolution.

One of the points of my paper is that European civilization during the years of the Renaissance developed an individualistic conception of man based upon the idea that each individual according to his sovereign will could not only affect nature but also his relations with other people by consent. That analytical and relationistic conception of man and nature was the precondition for science and technology but as well in the social and legal field the concept of contract as the justification of political democracy in the social contract and of private contract as the device for circulation of goods and other values. Thus, when the conception of human and subjective rights: i.e. *spheres of inviolable, legally protected and purely formal positions of integrity*, was accepted, only legal procedures were acceptable as solutions of legal conflicts. Japan, on the other hand, had kept her traditional collectivistic or organic structure of society and conception of man with its administrative conflict solutions, which, on the one hand, favours the protection of social interests, but on the other hand reduces the predictability of the outcome.

The social foundation of an individualistic contract thinking must of course be a society of some degree of strategic equilibrium between the individuals which, however, never became a reality but instead an illusion when evolution turned the population into producers and consumers. Of course, there was also in Europe the same need for protecting the social interests as there was in Japan. Japan received the European contract law, but - as Professor Kitagawa points out - changed it according to her own traditions of administrative conflict solution, so that conflicts are avoided by voluntary compliance with the so-called »guide lines« censoring the contract conditions of the various industries. According to their traditions Europeans generally used legislative and judicial procedures in fighting unfair contract conditions. But - as professor Kitagawa mentioned - the results according to general principles of comparative law tended to concur, with the exception, perhaps, that the legal position of - especially a foreign - individual is not so transparent in Japan as it is in Europe. Legal solutions increase predictability but might decrease protection, whereas administrative solutions decrease predictability but increase protection.

Now I shall turn to my paper about the general idea and function of contract. My analysis separates a *material* justification from a *formal* justification. The material justification is found in *reciprocity*, the formal one in *consent*. You may also

130

speak about a *functional* approach and an *ideological* approach. As it appears from the introductory legal anthropological remarks, the former might be regarded to be the elder one.

Men have at all times needed to exchange things and services with one another. Reciprocity is thus a logically necessary part of an exchange relation.

Anthropology teaches us that man is a social being in the sense that the human race would not be able to survive if there was not a social organization ensuring that the children could survive in spite of their helplessness during the first years of their lives. The price of developing a brain capacity like the one of *homo sapiens* is that the fetus has to leave the womb so early that the rest of the development into an independent individual has to take place outside the womb. According to anthropologists the female pelvis cannot be dimensioned larger than the actual size. The relation between the size of the head and thus the brain capacity and the pelvic region has remained unchanged throughout homo sapiens' hundreds of thousands years' history.

Therefore, in order to secure the survival of the children there has to be a minimum of *social organization* ensuring the division of labour which enables the mothers (or others) to rear the children while others provide food and protection. The smallest *social unit* is probably the nuclear family, father, mother and children, but the smallest social organization known from so-called primitive peoples in historical times is rather a family group of 30-50 persons.[1]

The behaviour of social species of animal is governed by *instincts*, i.e coded and unchangeable behaviour patterns, whereas man, who has an extreme paucity of instincts, is endowed with a brain capacity enabling him to control his behaviour through representative *ideas,* consciousness. The social needs are thus represented by moral and legal ideas, which are the foundation of the existence of the *small society* and at the same time the condition of the development of the *great society*.[2] Precisely because of his paucity of instincts man can easily adapt himself to the cultural development, which the cerebrum has enabled him to make.

We still do not know, however, why man lived under almost constant cultural conditions as food-gatherers and hunters for hundreds of thousands of years, and why about 10,000 years ago a dynamic development started, which at a still increasing speed has brought humanity to the highly technological society of today. However, doubtlessly it has something to do with the development of the agricultural technology, which permitted man to become resident and to make the economic surplus, which on the other hand was the condition of the extension of the superior form of organization with more division of labour liberating labour for abstract tasks.

The beginning of this development must also have something to do with essential changes of man's world of ideas and of his language, which is the medium, by means of which the thoughts are expressed. The human cerebrum and particularly the lobes of the brain developed rapidly nearly half a million years ago and have since then been unchanged. That is to say that the brain already at that time has had the capacity to make the ideas and the culture which, however, did not begin until several hundreds of thousands of years later. Why it did not start long before, and why it did start about 10,000 years ago in the Middle East, we do not know.

Modern anthropology and archaeological research finds that the climatic changes at the end of the latest Glacial Age are of great importance. The desiccation of areas in Africa and the Middle East decimated the amount of prey, while at the same time there were wild cereals, which might be grown, and animals, such as goats, sheep, dogs and so on, which might be tamed. However, these conditions have no doubt existed elsewhere and at other times without starting the development. On the other hand, it is good old learning that necessity is the mother of invention.

However that may be, the development started because the outward conditions were present, and because man had an enormous unused brain capacity[3] and a linguistic faculty, which also had unlimited potentialities.

Anthropologists warn us against considering present »primitive« peoples as preliminary stages of our present cultures and against using the *concept of development* as a scheme of interpretation for the description of our history at all. The known »primitive« cultures in our time have as a rule lived under so extreme circumstances that it is absurd to consider their cultures as a valid manifestation of the preliminary stage of mankind. Although it is self-evident that the concept of development is an ideological construction, the purpose of which is subsequently to justify what has actually happened and to make this understandable, and even though we shall never be able to *prove* that a certain development is *necessary*, it is not sufficient to make us reject the idea of development in history and (social) anthropology.

The concept of development can - like the concept of causation - not be proved. Already Hume demonstrated that it cannot be proved, as it is impossible to base necessity on empirical experiences. Necessity exists only in the world of thought, and as Kant established, this thought is on the other hand a condition - or category - of cognition and understanding in the same way as the conception of time and space. I have myself on another occasion maintained that it is similar with *the general prevention*, which claims that rules of sanction prevent people from doing forbidden things. If a certain amount of freedom of action was not presupposed the concept of responsibility was absurd, which was also realized by Kant,

132

and if these concepts were not presupposed it was absurd to make rules and sanctions at all.[4]

In the same way the concept of development must be a condition of cognition, if we shall altogether be able to make a subsequent description of historical matters. We must respect the fact that on the one hand archaeology and anthropology point out certain »primitive« cultures in the past, and that on the other hand we observe certain »advanced« cultures in the present. Culture has thus changed, and it is this change that we must call development. This does not imply any acceptance of a certain current theory of development, according to which what actually happens is bound to take place, but on the other hand it is an acknowledgement of the fact that certain traits of development are universal. There is no necessity for instance of a Marxist process of development from »primitive« via »feudal« and »capitalist« to »socialist« social systems. Experience shows this to perfection. However, there seems to be a fundamental difference *between* the »concrete« thinking and the »collective« conception of man in »primitive« cultures *and* the »abstract« thinking and »individualized« conception of man in urbanized cultures.

Not only *developmental psychology* speaks in favour of the idea that the development of each individual takes place in this way, but also legal history speaks in favour of such a »development« of social life, and maintains that it is not a question of influence but of »parallel courses«, although the tempo of development varies.[5] For instance, the fact that Japan has more easily managed to control the technological development with its highly developed organization may probably be due to the Japanese culture not yet having developed the individualistic conception of man, which together with Christianity was introduced into the Western World during the Renaissance, and which was in full bloom in the 19th century. On this basis the Western technology was created, which came to change society so thoroughly in a new »collective« direction that the representative »democracy« found it difficult to manage the governing function, while the more collective conception of man and society of Japan corresponded exactly to the needs of technology.[6]

I have in several of my earlier works[7] developed the conception *that* the contract as a fully developed idea belongs to a later time, *that* it is inseparably bound up with the idea of individual responsibility for tortious acts, and *that* this ideology from a breakthrough in the Mediterranean cultures during the 5th century B.C. through various stages of development arrived at its apotheosis from the middle of the 18th century to the middle of the 19th century. The technological development created from that time new forms of production, which by means of mass production have resulted in large-scale operations and large-scale marketing which had to be calculated and financed, so that there was no longer room for the individual responsibility and the individual contract.

All over the world the general *culpa-rule* (negligence) presupposing individual culpability as the condition of the liability for damages was replaced by an enterprise liability either in the form of a strict liability, like for instance for the railways, or a liability of factory owners for the errors committed by their workers, gradually often in the form of a »presumptive liability«, i.e. presumed negligence of the factory as a whole. At the same time the individual conception of contract is rejected, i.e. the combination of the free will of two individuals in favour of the *standard contract* presupposing that the individuals have counted on the *normal* market conditions unless explicit exception has been made.

And by this the ring is closed. We approach the thinking which originally dominated the exchange of goods and services, *the idea of equivalence*. The binding element is the receipt of a tender, for which you »owe« a consideration. The direct exchange between two persons both being present is no doubt the original one, at any rate it is the most simple form of voluntary exchange of goods and services. Outside the nearest family circle there will naturally be a difference between voluntary exchange of services (and goods) and involuntary deprivation of goods which are not unlimited. If there is an unlimited access to a resource, e.g. air, there will be no competition and no compulsory or voluntary surrender of goods. It appears from anthropological descriptions of primitive cultures that the balance between violence and mutual interest can be fragile. The various tribal societies, at the same time competing for and combining the utilization of external goods and their own products, have established »pre-contractual« exchange relations without direct contact. For instance members of one tribe have placed their surplus products in a certain place, whereupon they have retired. When they returned at a later date, they have found either their own goods or some other goods as payment. In the former case there has been made no »contract«, but in the latter case the parties have entered into a contract. Thus in their common interest they have replaced mutual competition by a mutual satisfaction of needs by voluntary means. At later stages they have met face to face and have directly exchanged goods and services in the market place or over the counter (bar).

To this operation are attached the representative ideas of tender and consideration, *the justice of equivalence*, which implies that it is the receipt of a tender that brings about *the obligation*, which is *equivalent* to the thing received. Even *Aristotle* emphasized the justice of equivalence, the *commutative* and equalizing justice, as the oldest and most fundamental one, while the *distributive* justice is a later addition, which arose at the time of Solon as a manifestation of the importance of

134

individuals and tenders to the emerging city-state. The equalizing justice has two main elements: The demand of criminal law for proportionality between crime and sentence (in contrast to the unlimited revenge of earlier times), and the demand of private law for accordance between the value of the tender and the consideration.

However, also legal history and culture history bear witness of the fundamental idea that the receipt of a tender binds the recipient to give a consideration. It is not the will but the receipt that establishes the obligation, even if the receipt is involuntary. The Icelandic writer *Halldor Laxness* gives an illustrating example in his novel: »Frie mænd« (Free Men). A peasant family in the wilds is in want and desperately needs the help of an enchantress. When she accepts an invitation she is offered some food, which she, however, refuses. Then the peasant catches her and feeds her forcibly. The fact is that she is now »obliged« to help him, as she has actually received a tender. However, she is as cunning as the peasant, and she goes outside and vomits. Then she is released from her obligation, and the peasant gets no help.

However, there are innumerable examples of this kind of thinking, a.o. also within legal history. In Greek law it was the receipt of deposits, arha, which established and thus were a condition of the obligation; and also within Roman law there had to be a *causa* in the form of a *real contract* or a *consensual contract*, corresponding to certain socio-typical relations: purchase, leasing, agency and so on, unless there was a formal *stipulation*. The purely informal, written or oral promise was not binding, especially not in case of unilateral dispositions (gifts). In general this is still the situation in European mediaeval law, in the legislation and legal usage as well as in the legal theory, which on the whole was based on the Romanistic tradition after the discovery of the Digests and Aristotle's writings in the 12th century. While the temporal Romanism (glossators, commentators, systematists) continued along this line, it was the catholic *moral philosophy* which prepared the later theory of contract. This theory had its most abstract version in Grotius (1625), who citing antique and ecclesiastical authorities claimed that two men as well as two states must be bound by their mutual promises, as by these they had each deposited a *particle of freedom* with the other, and thus had bound their will.

In the following centuries, concurrently with the growing prosperity in the cities, this type of contract came to prepare the way for new informal kinds of contracts during the transformation of the societies taking place at that time. However, within English law it was maintained that one was not obliged because one had made a declaration of intention, but because one had made a *bargain*.[8] The starting point was in the Middle Ages the same as on the Continent. One was bound, if certain formal rules *(seal)* were fulfilled. These formalities ensured *consideration* and *evidence;* among other things donatio mortis causa had to be secured by will, which was authorized by canon law as an intervention in the traditional law of family succession in order to secure property and other values to churches and convents as frankalmoins. Otherwise a person could be bound only in case of a special claim *(writ)* like in Roman law *(actio)*, i.e. the most common socio-typical relations between two parties. However, on the basis of a special fictional technique (assumpsit) a further development took place during the 16th century. By this English contract law was released from its traditional patterns, but at the same time the connection to the fundamental idea of the oldest contract law was maintained through the doctrine of *consideration*. The original meaning of »consideration« is reflection, but it got the technical meaning to combine the old doctrine of obligation by seal with an informal business practice, as it laid down as its only condition of the existence of consideration that the promisee had imposed a detriment on himself, or that the promisor had received a benefit. In other words there had to be a *quid pro quo*.[9] The purpose was naturally to ensure equivalence between tender and consideration like in the medieval Continental doctrine of *justum pretium*, but gradually it became a mere formality.

However, ideologically the doctrine has roots in common with the Continental natural law, which was developed by Grotius, Pufendorf, Thomasius and Wolff in the 18th century. It is true that this, according to Grotius' teaching, acknowledged the accepted promise as binding irrespective of its form and the unilaterality of the obligation. But if it was a mutually binding contract, the connection between tender and consideration was maintained, so that annulment or reduction of the tender or the consideration entitled the other party to cancel his obligation wholly or partly, for »one shall not give more than one gets« as a contemporary Danish writer expressed himself.[10] This form of the *idea of equivalence* came to influence commercial law and civil law on the whole a great deal, as the traditional Romanistic theory demanded that one party's non-fulfillment of his obligation had consequences only when there was culpa on the part of the non-fulfilling party. *Actio redhibitoria* and *actio quanti minoris* (annulment and proportional reduction of one's own tender because of defects) originally applied only to market trade, and at any rate only to the contract of sale. Therefore, for instance, there does not exist this very day in German law a general rule of annulment and reduction as the BGB is based on the Romance tradition of *culpa* (negligence) as the condition of liability, whereas the HGB contains such rules for commercial sale. On the other hand, for instance Danish private law practice and theory already at the end of the last century accepted such a fundamental connection between tender and consideration, though naturally with some modification.

However, by this we have already anticipated the development, which took place at different times within different legal systems. The development of trade necessitating credit facilities established *the claim* as a substitute for the goods or services received on credit. On the other hand *the debtor* in Roman law and in other known legal systems was personally bound in a literal sense. *Obligare* means linguistically to bind and *nexum* means to connect, and the conception corresponded to the fact that the debtor, in case he did not fulfil his obligation, was literally at the mercy of the creditor, as the creditor could kill him or sell him into slavery. In this way the connection between tender and consideration was preserved in an abstract form, a development, which corresponds to the magic ideas of a religious or moral obligation, which is known from other cultures. In the growing distant trade of the Middle Ages and the Renaissance it was originally the merchant himself who travelled along with his commodities by ship or in other ways, in order partly to protect the values in transit and partly to be in charge of the sale at the destination. Later on, when the princes undertook the job of securing the trade routes in return for payment of a duty, private protection was no longer necessary. According to modern history this was an essential economic background for the establishment of secular organizations, which were above the traditional family unit.

Another practical result of this development was the creation of the idea of representation and agency,[11] which meant that an intermediary - skipper, agent and so on - could make rights and obligations *in the name of another person*. This development implied also *money economy*, consisting in *an abstract measure of value:* at first fungible things (pecunia: cattle), then metal (copper, silver, gold) and coins (metal bearing the prince's stamp), later on notes, bills and other orders including other claims for money, which in the later stages imply confidence in the political organization guaranteeing the economy and issuing the means of payment.

According to culture history and philology the idea of money[12] in an abstract sense arose in Athens at the time of Solon (6th century B.C.) in the same period as other abstract ideas, such as *good, justice* in a distributive sense, *individual, democracy*. For during this period arose with its good or bad qualities an advanced city-culture based on an actual division of labour and the necessity of a new instrument for the organization of the economic and political function. The economies of earlier times, hunting, nomadic and agricultural economies, are collective, as all the individuals take part in the economic process, which in return ensures the individuals a share of the yield dependent on *their social status*. Everybody had a function, not only the young and strong people; the older people represent experience, which is of great importance in a *static* society, while the children represent future labour, and the social thinking is thus *conservative* and *dynastic*, i.e. the present generation represents the family or the people, which is the spiritual foundation indentifying the individuals with the past and the future.

Besides rendering it possible to make a surplus in the economy, a capital, the division of labour also creates a need for new *moral* and *legal* concepts, and thus also for a new political organization. When *labour* is priced (in money) then the old and the young people have no value. In a *dynamic* society the experience of the old people has no particular value, as it becomes antiquated, and the young people is also an economic burden, as they neither at the present nor if ever represent any contribution to the economy of the parents. The individualistic economy creates a *need* for a new morality, which by means of mercy as a religious demand creates the foundation of existence for the weak and ineffective people.[13] This revolution takes place gradually at the time between 450 B.C. and up to the birth of Christ, when it penetrated linguistically and culturally first in Palestine, later on in Greece and Italy.

The *legal* innovation is as mentioned *the contract* as a pattern of binding individuals and individual responsibility. Politically the idea of the individual as a sovereign rational being results in *the social contract*,[14] which by analogy with the private contract conceives society as an agreement among the citizens about governing society together. These thoughts were developed by *the Sophists* in Athens in the 5th century B.C. »Just as it is not the gods who created man, but the other way round, so it is not the gods, but man who made the laws«. This idea of democracy founding its binding force on a »social contract« emerges later on in the 17th century, when Europe has again established the economic foundation for an urbanized money economy based on the division of labour. At the beginning of the 17th century *Hugo Grotius* revives the idea, which is adopted by the contemporary *Hobbes*, but with quite another content. While Grotius builds on the anthropology of Aristotle and the Catholic moral philosophy, according to which man is a social being (zoon politikon), Hobbes was the first to consider man completely as a sovereign individual, however without any natural morality. While Grotius in a way considered man as social, Hobbes considered man as selfish and anti-social, and this is why he (man) in self-defence towards the other wolves entrusts his sovereignty to a prince, who autocratically will see to it that the individuals keep peace. Hobbes' political background was England, which was threatened by civil war, whereas Grotius partly agitated in favour of justifying the independence of the Netherlands of the Spanish ascendancy.

The social contract has in later theory been applied to representative democracy (Locke, Montesquieu, Kant, Fichte) as well as to direct democracy (Rousseau), and in recent times the idea has got new content in John Rawls' theory about the just society.[15]

After this incursion into legal and cultural history I should like to pause and have a look at the legal and moral philosophical analysis of the contract as a pattern of binding individuals. What is it that makes good the binding effect of the contract?

Modern *moral philosophy* as well as *economic theory* sometimes presuppose what is to be made good, namely that a contract is binding. John Rawls, for instance, bases the whole of his *moral* and *political* theory of justice on the assumption that the social contract is binding. Also economic theory since Adam Smith and up to the present time presupposes in its market economic foundation that the citizens' contracts are binding. However, it is an accepted fact within *legal theory* since the middle of the last century that it is not the contract alone as a declaration of intention, which is the binding cause but the power which derives from the rules of *the legislation* and thus again from the *political* organization of the state, as law and state according to a positivist as well as a Marxist interpretation are two sides of the same question. This combination of legal theoretical, economic and political premises has found a concise expression in *F. A. Hayek*'s social theory taking as its starting point a politico-legal analysis of the needs of modern society.[16] In a highly developed society, »the great society«, based on an extremely specialized technology and division of labour, there is a need for a politico-legal organization constituting two sides of the same question. At a very abstract level this organization is to take care of the communication, which in the most efficient way develops the resources of society and distributes the profit in the form of consumption and investment. Hayek rejects an intellectually »*governed*« model, for instance socialism, which results in inefficiency and bureaucracy, and a *natural* model, as the very civilization consists in the repression of natural needs in the »small« society (solidarity, loyality, equality) corresponding to the feelings which are built-in the biological code being unchanged since the rise of homo sapiens.

Hayek sees like *Hume*[17] three fundamental social laws:

            1) stability in property
            2) transfer by »consent«
            3) fulfilment of promises.

Economy is not the fundamental thing but is derived from the legal/political organization.[18] The market mechanism, which can be considered as the abstract and pluralistic and thus anonymous mechanism of distribution and priorities, must be placed on an equal footing with rules of law, which make and guarantee general expectations, the individual freedom and equal possibilities of the individuals.

This unreserved approval of liberal democracy has to be made with certain reservations. However, the theoretical content is essential. In the first place it is important to establish that the economic system derives from the legal and the political systems and not the other way round.[19] This is of importance to modern legal science, which has been using economic arguments, for instance the law of torts and the environmental law. Secondly *the consideration of confidence*, i.e. consideration of the fact *that* the individuals trust each other, and *that* the individuals *can* trust each other, is emphasized as the fundamental condition of the existence of any organized society. Without mutual confidence one cannot plan one's own conduct. Thus, the demand for truth has at all times been one of the most important *moral commandments*. It is one of the The Ten Commandments of Christianity, but forms a part of the »minimum content of law«, which *Herbert Hart* stresses as »descriptive natural law« for all cultures, and which *K. E. Løgstrup,* the Danish moralist, groups with the »sovereign manifestations of life« belonging to human nature.[20]

It is no mere coincidence that the considerations of truth and confidence are emphasized as social conditions as well as the basis of a private and political theory of organization. Any social theory is based on a conception of man (anthropology). A social theory and an »economic« organization based on the contract model conceive human beings as *individuals* with a rational will, which holds them responsible for the consequences of their actions, including their declarations of intention, and which therefore also ascribes a binding effect to the contract, thus establishing the necessary confidence.

Whether this or that anthropology is the »right« one, we - as already mentioned - do not know for sure, and the question may be absurd, as man's paucity of instincts may be the reason why he can adapt himself to all outward forms of organization necessitated by the culture that he has created. Perhaps it is correct, as found by Aristotle, that man is indeed a social animal but that the political forms of government, monarchy, oligarchy and democracy,[21] are nothing but different types corresponding to different needs under changing circumstances.

However, extreme individualism and extreme collectivism are probably forms of fantasy rather than forms of reality. In real life the organization must be adapted to the balancing of, on the one hand, the individuals' egoistic interests and, on the other, of the superior objects of the social organization. The *commutative* and the *distributive* justice have to compete in the same way as the need for freedom and security and the need for an exchange of goods and services on the basis of *contract* and *status*.[22]

Finally I should like to make some remarks about the influence of the idea of contract on the institution of marriage.[23] Also here it is essential to emphasize the two important but different elements of the contract: the *material* principle of equivalence and the *formal* principle of consensus.

While the material element dominates under *primitive* social conditions, where the family and the property of the family - primarily its landed property - are the predominant interests, the formal element becomes prevalent from the breakthrough of urbanization in Europe in the 16th and 17th centuries.

However, already in classical Rome the institution of marriage had become an informal, terminable contract between the parties. Together with the disruption of the Roman Empire the institution of marriage changed again into the old private status relations, but the Church came gradually to play a more important part, until the development turned in the 17th century.

Within the old agrarian societies based on the family, which arose again, it is up to the family to choose the persons to carry on the family through marriage and procreation of children. This is the reason why the contract is not made between the individuals, but between the heads of the families, often while the persons in question are still children, either as children's marriages - within certain cultures - or, like in Europe, normally as *betrothal*, an agreement about future marriage.

Until the 16th century the Church had to accept that marriage was a temporal institution and that it could even be made by an informal contract between the parties in connection with sexual intercourse. Hereby arose an intermediate form between the old material and the more recent formal idea of marriage, probably with the original purpose of ensuring that children born by parents cohabiting against the will of the family should not be illegitimate like children from promiscuous relations. In the 16th century the *church wedding* becomes a condition of the validity of the marriage in Catholic as well as in Protestant countries, but the formal element of the contract, consensus, becomes to an increasing extent instructive to the concept of marriage together with the rationalistic natural law thought in the 17th and 18th centuries. This applies to the institution of marriage as well as to the arrangement - in regard to the law of property - which can be made according to a marriage settlement. Besides it applies to the institution of separation and divorce which began to evolve in Protestant countries. Altogether, within the natural law theory the institution of marriage is conceived as a contract in regard to the law of property to such a degree that infidelity is considered to be at variance with the establishment of the contract of an exclusive *ius reale personale* (Kant) with a mutual right of use.

This development reflects the development in labour relations, which as mentioned above, like other legal matters in regard to the law of property develop from status into contract (Maine). As I have pointed out the trend since the middle of the last century has been towards status relations, this applies with special force to labour contracts, which on the one hand are based on collective agreements and on the other hand to an increasing extent have been made irrevocable.

Still, there is a certain irony in the fact that the institution of marriage has continued the development towards a purely contractual level. In today's Denmark less than half of the couples living permanently together has formalized their relationship through marriage. The majority is based solely on a written or unwritten agreement, which can freely be terminated with the consequences that it will have for the distribution of the children (who are considered to be unconjugal and therefore are given to the mother), and the mixed property, which, however, is divided either according to the agreement or if such one does not exist on an estimate.

The cause of this development must be found in the social development which has involved women in trade, and which has therefore gradually adapted the tax system and the social system to this fact, with the result that the parties are no longer treated economically and socially as a family, but as two individuals. In several countries - most extreme in Sweden - the marriage acts have been changed in such a way that they approach the reality of the informal marriage, like a contract which can freely be made and terminated without very heavy economic or social consequences. By this I have said nothing about the situation of the children and thus of the next generation.

Notes

1) See on the latest legal biological research, *Werner Schurig*, Überlegungen zum Einfluss biosoziologischer Strukturen auf das Rechtsverhalten (1983). See also *Julian Jaynes*, The Origin of Consciousness in the Breakdown of the Bicameral Mind (1976); *George Edgin Pugh*, The Biological Origin of Human Values (1978); *C. Owen Lovejoy*, The Origin of Man, Science, 211 (1981) p. 341 ff.; *Alois Troller*, Überall gültige Prinzipien der Rechtswissenschaft (1965); *Stig Jørgensen*, Pluralis Juris (1982), p. 36; *same*, Das Individuum, die Gesellschaft und das Widerstandsrecht, in: Osterreichische Zeitschrift für öffentliches Recht (1973), p. 19 ff.

2) See *F. A. Hayek*, Law, Legislation and Liberty, vol. 1-3 (1982). See also *P. S. Atiyah*, Promises, Morals and Law (1981), and *Stig Jørgensen*, Law and Society (1971) Ch. 2; *same*, Vertrag und Recht (1968) p. 13 ff. and 111 ff.; *same*, Contract as Form, in: Scan-

dinavian Studies in Law, vol. 10 (1966) p. 97 ff.; *same*, Ethik und Gerechtigkeit (1980); *same*, Values in Law (1978) p. 59 ff.; *same*, Pluralis Juris (l.c. note 1) p. 11 ff. See also *Conrad D. Johnson*, The Idea of Autonomy and the Foundation of Contractual Liability, Law and Philosophy, vol. 2 (1983), p. 271 ff.

3) Modern brain physiology has shown that the forebrain has no specific function, like the cerebellum and other parts of the cerebrum, and therefore is important for refined feelings and thoughts.

4) *Stig Jørgensen,* Johs. Andenæs og almenpræventionen, in: Lov og frihet, Festskrift til Johs. Andenæs (1982) p. 175 ff.

5) *Stig Jørgensen,* Law and Society (l.c. note 2) Ch. 2; *same*, Ethik und Gerechtigkeit (l.c. note 2) p. 12 ff. and 30 ff.; *same*, Values in Law (l.c. note 2) p. 65 ff.; Pluralis Juris (l.c. note 2) p. 21 ff.; *same*, Vertrag und Recht (l.c. note 2) p. 13 ff. Already the Italian philosopher *Giambattista Vico* (1668-1744) presupposed such a parallel concept of development and connected it with a theory of development for the social organization from a »religious« via an »authoritarian« to a »human« stage, cf. *Aristotle:* monarchical, oligarchical and democratic; and *Max Weber,* Wirtschaft und Gesellschaft (1964) p. 26 ff. (traditionelle, charismatische und rationale Legitimität).

6) See on Japanese development of the law, *Paul Eubel und andere,* Das japanische Rechtssystem (1979); about the reception of European civil law in Japan: *Z. Kitagawa,* Europäisches Zivilrecht in Japan (1970) and Rezeption und Fortbildung des europäischen Zivilrechts in Japan, in: Arbeiten zur Rechtsvergleichung, hrsg. von H. Dölle und E. v. Caemmerer (1970) p. 221 ff.; see also *same*, Resonance Theory. A Tentative Approach to the Dispute Settlement Mechanism, in: Rechtsvergleichung, Europarecht und Staatsintegration, Gedächtnisschrift für L.-J. Constantinesco, hrsg. von Gerh. Lüke und andere (1983) p. 393 ff. On the explanations of the falling criminality in Japan, see *Robert B. McKay,* Japan: Streets without Crime. Dispute without Lawyers, in: Japan House Newsletter, vol. XXIV, No. 9 (New York 1977); and *Johs. Andenæs,* Kriminalitet og økonomisk utvikling. Et japansk under, in: Lov og rett (1979) p. 464 ff. In all cases it is tried to limit the level of conflict through an unofficial group control and unofficial non-legal procedures of solving the conflicts based on acceptance on the part of the family and other social and occupational units. See also *José Llompart,* Rechtsbewusstsein und Verantwortungsgefühl im Japan der Gegenwart, Rechtstheorie, 14 (1983), p. 285 ff.; *Mitsukuni Yasaki,* Significance of »Legal Consciousness« in regard to Social Facts and Social Institutions, Osaka University Law Review, 31 (1984), p. 1; *Manfred Rehbinder,* Die Rezeption fremden Rechts in soziologischer Sicht, Rechtstheorie, 14 (1983) p. 305 (Korea).

7) See above note 2.

8) *Atiyah*, (l.c. note 2); Stig Jørgensen, 4 obligationsretlige afhandlinger (1965) p. 17 ff.

9) *Stig Jørgensen,* Values in Law (l.c. note 2) p. 69 ff.

10) *Stig Jørgensen,* Die skandinavische Lehre der Vertragsverletzung, in: Festschrift für Karl Larenz (1973), p. 549 ff.

11) *Stig Jørgensen,* Fuldmagtsproblemer, in: Juristen (1968) p. 401 ff.

12) See to the following, *Stig Jørgensen,* Ethik und Gerechtigkeit (l.c. note 2) p. 15; *same*, Pluralis Juris (l.c. note 2) p. 21 ff. See on the development of the concepts »subjective law«, »individual«, »person«, »responsibility«, »conscience« which were not to be

found in Japanese culture and law when European law was received in this century; *José Llompart* (l.c. note 6).

13) *Stig Jørgensen*, Ethik und Gerechtigkeit (l.c. note 2) p. 12 ff.

14) *Stig Jørgensen*, Values in Law (l.c. note 2) p. 69 ff., p. 73 ff. and p. 103 ff.; *same*, Ethik und Gerechtigkeit (l.c. note 2) p. 37 ff.

15) *Stig Jørgensen*, Pluralis Juris (l.c. note 2) p. 24 ff.; *same*, Ethik und Gerechtigkeit (l.c. note 2) p. 37 ff.

16) See above note 2.

17) *Hayek*, Law, Legislation and Liberty (l.c. note 2) vol. 2, p. 40.

18) *Stig Jørgensen*, Der Begriff des Eigentums in geschichtlicher und gegenwärtiger Betrachtung, in: Festschrift für Helmut Schelsky (1978) p. 249 ff.

19) Adam Smith's economic theory was part of his social and legal philosophy; see *Peter Stein*, Adam Smith's Jurisprudence between Morality and Economics, in: Cornell Law Review (1979) p. 622 ff.; *P. Winch*, Science and the Legislator: Adam Smith and after, in: The Economic Journal, vol. 93 (1983) p. 501 ff.; see also *Paul Burrows* and *Cento G. Veljanovski*, The Economic Approach to Law (1981) p. 1 ff.; *Robert E. Lane*, Individualism and the Market Society, in: Nomos XXV (1983) (Liberal Democracy, ed. by *J. R. Pennock* and *J. W. Chapman*); Rational Man and Irrational Society? ed. by *Brian Barry* and *Russell Hardin* (1982); *Mortimer R. Kadish*, Practice and Paradox. A Comment on Social Choice Theory, in: Ethics, vol. 90 (1983) p. 680; Philosophy of Economics, ed. by *W. Stegmüller* and *W. Balzer*; *W. Spohn*, Studies in Contemporary Economics (1982); *Stig Jørgensen*, Pluralis Juris (l.c. note 2) p. 24 ff.

20) *Sissela Bok*, Lying, Moral Choice in Public and Private Life (1978).

21) *Stig Jørgensen*, Demokratie und Völkerbewegung, in: Filisofia del Derecho y Filosofia Politica, X Weltkongress der IVR, vol. III (1981) p. 83 ff.

22) See also *Stig Jørgensen*, Contract as Form (l.c. note 2) and *V. Aubert*, In Search of Law (1983) p. 115 f.; *W. Schmidt*, Zur sozialen Wirklichkeit des Vertrages (1983).

23) See *Mary Ann Glendon*, State, Law and Family (1977) Ch. 7.

The Crisis of Democracy

I. The Jurist as a Social Analyst

Why is it that the jurist has something special to give as a social analyst and social commentator? The problem may be illustrated by some experiences of a cross-scientific study group within the Faculty of Social Sciences at Aarhus University.[1]

The other social sciences - Economics, Politics, and Psychology - have so far tended to consider their functions and models as a priori in the sense that the real society must be organized in accordance with a certain degree of efficiency which results from their (i.e. the above mentioned sciences) criteria of rationality. However, it has appeared from this cooperation that the functions of the other sciences depend on the existence of a legal organization and government. The economists' market economic models have naturally no validity without a pre-existing rule about agreements being binding. In the same way our statistic and mathematic basis has turned out to be influenced by the particular and causal arrangement of the natural sciences to a far too high degree, whereas the social relations cannot be dealt with without considering the pre-existing social structure and social institutions. Thus, the elements in society being studied cannot be considered as isolated islands, for man is, as expressed by the ancient natural law theorists from Aristotle to Grotius and Pufendorf, a rational being as well as a social being (zoon politikon). As we shall see, this is rather important to the conclusions that we may draw from the various theories and models which have arosen within social theory.

What characterizes the jurist's consideration of society compared to that of other scientists?: (1) Legal science stresses that things should be governed by norms and rules, whereas the empiric social sciences and the natural sciences favour the functional considerations of efficiency. (2) Compared to the traditionally individualizing and concretizing consideration of the humanist, the jurist has been educated to consider the individual case as an element of a fundamental general relation. While the humanist is inclined to consider the individual case as unique and therefore take a corresponding position on concrete problems, the jurist has learned to understand that a solution of a problem does not aim only at finding the concrete just result, but also has to take into consideration that the concrete decision is to appear as a guide to future decisions in similar cases.

The jurist's ability to consider each concrete case from a theoretical point of view has always been characteristic of the juridical function. Evidently, no organized cooperation among people can exist without rules, making the behaviour of other people predictable. Trust in one another has always been a fundamental thing in morality. The same is true of the demand for truth. On the other hand it is self-evident that predictability implies an already known system of norms and rules, making it possible to make prognoses or predictions of the behaviour of other human beings. Equality, that is here to say the regard for equal cases being treated equally, has from time immemorial been a crucial substance of the conception of justice of any society. However, the fact that equal cases are to be treated equally is only another way of saying that human behaviour should be governed by rules. Arbitrariness has always been held to be unjust; the psychologist *Franz From* once assumed that crime is held to be negative because, and exactly because, it is a socially unpredictable behaviour. Therefore the criminal is considered to be guilty and is punished.

As the public debate has been reserved especially for humanists and others with a similar cultural background, and as the pre-existing tendency to concrete thinking is increased by a tendency encouraged by the mass media - especially in our time - to individualization, dramatization and fragmentation of the events of the day, it is quite natural that the public debate, seen through the eyes of jurists, seems odd, chaotic and inconsistent. After the Orwell-year »1984« there may be a special ground for drawing attention to the concept of doublethink, which Orwell found characteristic of modern man: the capability of thinking and believing one thing on the one hand and thinking and believing the opposite thing on the other without realizing that the ideas are self-contradictory. In my opinion this capability of doublethink is extremely well-developed in modern democracies. This capability is often confused with hypocrisy, which on the other hand implies consciousness of the discrepancy between the opposite opinions. But naturally it may be what jurists usually call dolus eventualis or intentional good faith. Pragmatism is often said to be the better part of valour. It is true that doctrinarianism leads to pedantry or madness, but pragmatism will often turn into unprincipled realism.

The reason why I will not - after all - deal particularly with Orwell's book is that his way of presenting the problems, which for natural reasons lay near at

146

hand in 1948, is no longer realistic. At that time the Iron Curtain had descended through Europe, and Stalin had initiated the Berlin Crisis, and it was therefore quite natural to see the threat to Western democracies as the spread of Soviet Communism to the West. The experiences of the past 35 years have clearly demonstrated that this threat is not the most serious one to Western democracies. Whether the peace movements like it or not, NATO, the atom bombs and the missiles have effectively prevented such a spread of the totalitarian state to Western Europe, no matter what wishes the leaders of Kremlin may have had in that respect.

Neither does the threat to democracy - as many have thought - come first and foremost from modern technology, including especially the technology concerning information and EDP. The risk that the technological development might lead to a centrally governed state is counteracted by the contrary possibilities of this technology, i.e. decentralization of not only the systems of production but also the systems of decision-making, which has in fact turned out to be the case. In my opinion the threat to Western democracies comes from the inside as a result of all the good things that the economic and cultural development of the past 150 years has built in society. It is a well-known fact that a great part of what has been meant to be philantropic has in its wider form turned out to be misantropic and bad. Just remember how the Inquisition, which for good Christian reasons was meant to prevent criminals from dying without having confessed their crimes, later on became an instrument of terror and torture towards innocent people. If we assume that democracy depends on a certain amount of prosperity and a certain standard of general education, the object of the democratic ideology must be and has also been to further the citizens' welfare and education: I shall try to demonstrate and prove that these actually good forces involve some bad forces, i.e. forces being incompatible with the idea and function of democracy.

Thus, while Orwell sees the risk of democracy in the trend of development towards a totalitarian state, experience shows, in my opinion, that the trend has instead been towards the uncontrollable society, because nobody has considered it his task to look after the interests of society as a whole. Instead interest groups and populistic movements have together with the mass media made it difficult to formulate the »rational common will«, of which first Aristotle and since several others have spoken.[2]

On the other hand socialism may not be the greatest threat to democracy. Many have rightly said that Soviet socialism has nothing to do with socialism, as real socialism has a humane face. The problem is only that such a socialism has never been brought into being on earth. Just as Winnie the Pooh found that the bees, humming around the nose of the cloud, were the wrong kind of bees and therefore made the wrong kind of honey, the Utopian socialists of the West have always had to realize that the existing socialist regimes do not represent the real kind of socialism. Below I shall return to the problem whether socialism and democracy are compatible, or whether democracy depends on an economic organization based on market economy and private property.[3]

II. Perspectives Concerning Legal History.
Collectivism - Individualism

However that may be, legal history can contribute to the understanding of Soviet socialism.[4] I think it was August Strindberg, who once ventured the disingenuity towards his own country to maintain that Asia begins in Malmö. Apart from the fact that Malmö is old Danish land there is in a figurative sense this amount of truth in his statement that Asia and Western Europe represent two different cultures. In other words Asia may be said to begin in Leningrad. The bearing of the statement is that only Western Europe on the basis of the Greek-Jewish culture in the Renaissance developed an individualistic philosophy of man based on the idea that the individual is the smallest unit of society, and that the individuals therefore have part in the sovereignty, which is the foundation of society and the authority for legislation. Thus democracy follows logically from this as the social order. Within this very period of time the Russian Empire was precluded from Western influence because of the Tartars' rule for more than 200 years. Although Peter the Great and other later Russian Tsars endeavoured to introduce Western culture into the Russian Empire, they never succeeded in overcoming the collectivistic philosophy of man, which is the foundation of all Asian (and African) cultures, including the Japanese culture. Even though considerable judicial reforms were carried through at the end of the last century, a fundamental distinction between a judicial and an administrative government was never established.

While the individualistic legal thought in Western Europe was based on the idea of subjective rights, which so to speak surrounded each individual with an inviolable sphere irrespective of the interests of society and the rulers, the Soviet Empire has always from the Tsarist period to the Soviet State maintained essential social tasks as administrative systems being subject to the freedom of disposal of the existing social authorities at the time in question. The fundamental basis for Western legal thought is that everybody may refer to a rule of law, if they comply with the formal criteria. Contrary to the religious or ideological systems in the east and the south it is not in principle possible to reserve the right to ideological, political or religious censorship of the formal contents of the rules. It is self-evident that a non-formal conception of law reduces the possibility of predictability in society, and the counterpart of this is haphazardness and lacking law and order, which is precisely what characterizes any regime of terror, whether it is well-meaning or not. All jurists will admit that at any rate the rules of commercial law cannot control a modern system of production, trade and credit without such clear, precise and formal rules of law. Without security in the turnover this system cannot function. For instance, nobody will give credit without being sure of payment at some future time, no matter whether the debtor is rich or poor, just or unjust.

In all primitive cultures the conception of man and society is collectivistic, objective, and casuistic.[5] It is not the individual but the clan, the tribe, the family which is the foundation of society. The values are distributed according to status relations, and the responsibility does not rest with the individuals, but with the family, and it is attached to the act and not to the offender's subjective conditions. In this connection it is natural to refer to the Old Testament. The conception of society in this nomadic culture is authoritarian and hierarchic. Honour God, the law and your parents. Breach of the law is met by an act of revenge, which in cases of minor offences is converted into a fine, while, moreover, the revenge is limited to the law of talion, an eye for an eye and a tooth for a tooth. On the other hand it is characteristic *that* the revenge is transmitted to the children until the seventh generation, and *that* the reaction does not depend on the guilt of the offender.

Professor E. Hammershaimb has analysed the development from the objective and collective conception of society and man of the Old Testament to the Christian individualism of the New Testament.[5] He demonstrates how a collective conception of society and man is changed into an individualistic one, linguistically as well as morally, during the 5th century after the return from the Babylonian Captivity and the meeting with the advanced trade and cities of the Palestinian coastal states. By the transition to the city-state with its division of labour and with its money economy the assets of society were no longer divided according to the status of the individual in the community, but according to his deserts. Hammershaimb shows how in a dynamic city culture children and old people are reduced to needless and worthless individuals, whereas in the previous static culture they represented the future maintenance and the highest wisdom respectively. A view which is still relevant. Therefore, Hammershaimb emphasizes, a new morality is needed, and it is precisely this new individualistic morality that is radicalized by Christ to the unreserved love of one's neighbour. As neighbour is stressed especially the children, the weak, the old and the helpless. At the same time stress is laid on the individual's subjective responsibility for his actions to God and man.

This transition from a collective nomadic and agrarian culture to a subjective city culture takes place at about the same time in other parts of the Mediterranean area. In Rome the power of the nobility or patriciers is shattered approximately 450 (B.C.) concurrently with the hanging of the Twelve Tables in Forum Romanum. As early as the 6th century (B.C.) Solon initiated the winding up of the power of the nobility and the introduction of partially democratic social systems, among other things by means of his debt and money reforms. However, the individualistic philosophy of man, the subjective responsibility and the fundamental democratic ideology evolve gradually. As late as in Aischylos' drama »Oresteia« about the middle of the 5th century (B.C.) the objective destined responsibility of the family recurs, whereas after the middle of the 5th century in Sofokles' »Antigone« the conception occurs that the individual is not responsible alone but may also refer to a higher natural law in defence of an action which usually is considered to be a crime. Exactly here in Perikles' flourishing Athens the so-called Sophists rejected a religious, metaphysical philosophy of life and society and claimed that man created the Gods and not the other way round, just as man created his own laws by convention. For the first time the social contract is used as the ideological basis of a democratic form of government. The government of society depends on and is derived from the citizens' free support of society by a collective agreement.

According to Plato and Aristotle the Peleponnesian wars demonstrated the moral weakness of unlimited democracy, and they therefore demanded reforms. While Plato, as we know, wanted to introduce a kind of Communist dictatorship governed by philosophers and protected by soldiers, the pedestrian Aristotle would use not quite as radical means for the retrieval of the faults of the unregulated and direct democracy. Here it is necessary to point out that in principle the decisions in Athens were made in great popular assemblies and that the decisions therefore were not made in accordance with fixed administrative or judicial rules. Therefore, it is a characteristic feature of the argumentation that it is politico-rhetorial and not juridical. In Athens they developed a rhetorical theory and practice, the very purpose of which were to induce a public assembly, whereas a legal expert knowledge and profession were unknown concepts until the later Roman culture, which to a far higher degree was based on an objective legal system.

Aristotle found that the system of government of the societies varies as to time, and that the respective systems of government have certain advantages and disadvantages dependent on the social conditions, to which they are attached. All of these three systems of government have a positive as well as a negative side. (1) Monarchies have - as indicated by the name - only one ruler, and the values are distributed according to status. (2) Oligarchies are governed by few people, and the values are distributed according to merits and achievements, whereas democracies are governed by people in general, and the values are distributed equally.

Aristotle considered, as mentioned, man as a rational and a social animal. As a nature-being he needs some organization and exchange of goods and services in order to manage the rearing of his children and the preservation of the human race, and as a rational being he is able to change his surroundings and create culture and social organization according to his various needs.

The negative variant of monarchy is tyranny, and the positive variant of oligarchy is aristocracy, which is the government of the best men. The negative side of democracy is vulgar democracy, which Aristotle thought to have experienced during the Peloponnesian wars. The foundation of society cannot and should not be the naked common will, if the object of society is to make all people happy. The good society can be realized only where there is a general law, and where this law is in accordance with *the rational common will*. Where the masses rule through unprincipled decisions, democracy is perverted to a vulgar democracy, because it is subject to demagoges seducing the people, just as the tyrants are seduced by flatterers.

Thus, the democratic form of government arose in the city-state together with the division of labour and a resulting money economy, which made possible an economic surplus as well as abstract relations between individuals by means of contracts, which again made possible the creation of abstract concepts, such as individual rights, duties and responsibility. Democracy disappears again as idea and phenomenon by the appearance of the great Mediterranean empires, first the Hellenistic Empire and later the Roman Empire. Together with the disruption of the Roman Empire Western culture and economy are fragmented, and the social systems return regressively to an agrarian economy and a feudal form of government. As substitute for the Roman emperor appeared the Pope as the spiritual and temporal authority on earth. Through the doctrine of the two swords Eusebius justified the division of the power into a temporal and a spiritual power with the Church as the superior authority legitimating the power of the prince by the grace of God. So the sovereignty and consequently the legislative power lie not with the temporal but with the spiritual authority.

Together with a new surplus in economy, first in the Northern Italian commercial centres, the state and legal thought began to develop again. Already during the first renaissance in the 13th century *Thomas Aquina* recognizes that temporal authorities have a certain legislative power within the limits of the principles being manifested in the divine and natural law. However, it was not until the following century that *Marsilius* of Padua and *Bodinius* justify the temporal legislative power with reference to the idea of sovereignty. Not until the 17th and 18th centuries - after a new surplus in economy resulting from the great discoveries - arises a renewed economic and cultural basis for the idea of democracy. *Grotius* and *Hobbes* were the first to revive the idea of the social contract in the middle of the 17th century. The social contract made Grotius defend democracy from an optimistic philosophy of man, whereas from a negative philosophy of man it made Hobbes defend despotism.

John Locke and *Montesquieu* adopted later on the individualistic philosophy of man which assumed that any human being is born free and equal with a right to defence and property. However, to a certain degree they accepted Hobbes' pessimism, finding that the power had a tendency to corrupt. For that reason they argued in favour of a splitting up of the power in society into a legislative, an executive and a judicial power controlling one another. They defended a representative democracy as well, in which the people was to elect qualified persons as its representatives in the legislature, whereas *Rousseau,* on the other hand, found that the sovereignty of the people was indivisible, but had to be united in »volonté generale«. The result was a kind of direct democracy like the one in antique Athens, and as the situation was in Rousseau's original native country Switzerland, where the small local areas are still governed by popular votes.

Kant's main problem after the French Revolution was how to combine the interests of the state with the real freedom of the individuals, and here he agreed with Aristotle that the state was to secure the sensible interests of the individuals in accordance with the general rules of law.

III. The Modern Dilemma

The problem of Aristotle, Rousseau and Kant was to safeguard the freedom of the individuals as well as the interests of society and not allow the particular interests of minorities to dominate or to be dominated. Aristotle spoke of a *general law,* Rousseau of the true *general interest*, and Kant of the *rational will*, but they all had the same thing in mind. In the light of some Danish experiences, which I find representative of Western societies, I shall try to show in the following how the development of the politico-economical system in our time tends towards a kind of corporate state, where the power is attached to great bureaucracies. These have arisen within the public as well as within the private sector, and together they constitute a joint concentration of power, as the state has assumed the responsibility for a great part of private economy, and private economy, on the other hand, has achieved great influence on the economic policy of the state through its organizations. Politicians, officials and representatives of trade unions and other professional and industrial bodies sit on committees, which prepare and administer a so-called delegated legislation. In this way the division of power in society has to a large degree become illusory.

On the other hand bureaucratization and centralization in society have created a kind of frustration, as the individuals feel that they do not understand what is going on, and that they have no real influence on political decisions. Thus we have seen that the confidence in political parties has fallen quickly with a drastic fall of the number of party members, while, on the other hand, the number of members of trade unions has increased enormously. These unions have taken over the material function of the political parties, and we experience how the idealistic function has been taken over by the so-called grass-roots movements or populistic parties working for liberty or for the quality of life, for instance for nature, a better environment, whales, for peace or against nuclear power stations, missiles, NATO, and the EEC. We saw how the so-called adolescent revolt flourished at the universities in the late 60s with demands for participation of the students in the administration of the universities and of the workers in the management of the industry. What was new about this was not only the programme but also the means, the non-acceptance of the rules of law, not only demonstrations, but also open disobedience and even violence.[6]

It had become obvious that the political process was not, as believed by the fathers of democracy in the Enlightenment, a rational debate among enlightened persons. Already at the end of the 19th century it had become clear that politics is a fight among different social interests, and that the court is the meeting place for such competing interests. However, the new electronic media made it possible to demonstrate these interests by means of spectacular events and happenings of any kind.

Concurrently with the economic recession that we have seen through the last decade it has become obvious that the tolerance of society has been reduced and that it is a question whether the democratic system is able to solve the great economic and social problems in a situation where the confidence of the people to a large degree has been with their trade unions and with aggressive populistic movements, which feel no responsibility for the interest of society, but consider their special interest as the most important one and sometimes as the only one. Now and then it has been called »the terror of the loudspeaking persons«. At any rate we have seen that the social solidarity in several fields collapses, and this is the reason why the law-abidingness has declined.

The problem is how to save democracy and maintain some fundamental elements of *the idea and practice of democracy: the struggle for making political decisions serve the public interests equally,* as formulated by Aristotle.

The American economist and Nobel Prize winner Kenneth Arrow has formulated the so-called »Arrow's theorem«, which apparently convincingly states that there exists no rational way, in which priority may be given to different values in a democratic system. On the other hand democracy is the only system which can give the government sufficient information about the real interests of the people.

If you like to express yourself in paradoxes, it can be said that *the demand for participation has reached a peak in a situation where society has become so complicated and the division of labour so inscrutable that the possibility of making meaningful contributions to the decision-making process has become insignificant.*

On the one hand there is the problem of *legitimation* of the political process demanding participation, and on the other hand the problem of *efficiency* demanding qualifications. The power of the people must be canalized into a responsible political and administrative work.

But the question is: How?

Implied in Arrow's theorem is an assumption that the solution is to be found in the dictatorship. However, Eastern European experiences have demonstrated that it was true - as a Polish professor said some years ago - that an economy controlled by the state is possible and sensible in cases of war, revolution and under the building up of the heavy industries. Besides market economy in some form is the only mechanism, which can ensure the producers sufficiently precise information about the needs of the population and the effective distribution of resources. This has also been realized in Yugoslavia and Hungary, where a kind of market economy has been introduced into formally Socialist social systems.

Here we face the main problem and perhaps also an indication of its solution: *the interdependence between economic pluralism and democracy, and between market mechanism and freedom.*

The progress of technology since World War I has created a need for national and international intervention of society in economy in order to create the conditions necessary for the production and trade. Society is responsible for the infrastructure: roads, railways, communication, education, and external and internal peace. An explanation of the crisis in the 30s is that the politicians in the 20s tried to return to normal after the wartime economy without having realized the fact concealed by the war that modern industry had become dependent on the public sector's regulation and stimulation of the purchasing power and investments in society.[7]

John Keynes' economic theory with this content was therefore used as a means of overcoming the crisis in the U.S.A. and Europe and as an economic and moral instrument for the creation of economic growth and greater equality through public consumption, investment, and saving up.

After World War II everything seemed to be going well, until the development left the track at the beginning of the 70s. Of couse the oil crisis had something to do with the new phenomenon called »stagflation« (stagnation and inflation at the same time), but only as the provoking factor. Underneath the material causes were already in full blast: The vicious spiral of wages and taxes, which to a high degree was due to the growing power of the trade unions on the one hand, and on the other the employers' willingness to pay higher wages rather than risking strikes and other interruptions of the production and consequently lose shares of the market. The employers could also to a large degree find the money for the increasing wages by means of rationalization and automation, which became profitable. The immediate result was a growing unemployment, but not a drastic reduction of the purchasing power, as the political system, which was also dominated by the trade organizations, ensured a high unemployment benefit, which was financed by the state through growing taxes, resulting in demands for higher wages, and so on.

In the meantime the whole society had become dependent on public funds. A growing part of the population is now employed within the public sector, which in Scandinavia together with the transfer of incomes to the public budgets is approx. 50 p.c. of the gross national product. The political system has had difficulty in making appreciable reductions in the public budgets. In principle most of the political parties have now recognized the need for such reductions, but when it comes to concrete proposals, they seem to have a tendency to vanish in the blue air, *because public expenditure always somewhere is private income for someone, and because private interests have been professionally organized and are able to mobilize the mass media in a campaign, while the public interest is abstract and weakly supported.* While we are dealing with paradoxes it should be mentioned that all opinion polls prove that also the population as a whole wants great retrenchments of the public budgets. When people thereafter are asked sector by sector, if this should be extended or reduced, the answers show that the same population wants to extend the public sector quite considerably.

In other words there has been a general tendency to make the private sector dependent on public subsidies of any kind. This means that still more of the decisions of society about the distribution of values become political in the sense that voting in principle is the criterion for distribution. The limits of this mechanism are stated in Arrow's theorem and are noticeable in our daily life, where the competition and the cooperation among the political parties, the organizations and the pressure groups until a couple of years ago incessantly stimulated the spiral.[8]

Another research project at our faculty seems to justify the statement that governments in democratic societies in general, and especially minority governments, have more or less been given the part of the auctioneer, who makes proposals, which are neutralized by different pressure groups.[9] Now, things are not always as black as they are painted. In the first place the statistics, on which Kenneth Arrow based his theorem, seem to assume that the individuals are particular and passive figures, like the elements in a scientific function. Arrow seems to overlook the fact that man on the one hand is a social being and on the other a rational being, who not only learns from his experiences, but also is able to make institutions and rules opposing the development, which threatens his existence. In fact a lot of things indicate that people in Western societies have now begun to realize that democratic forms of decision only to a limited extent can manage the distribution of values in society, if a minimum of efficiency and responsibility shall be preserved.[10] Coincident opinion polls in Holland and Denmark in the spring of 1982 demonstrated that in the populations as a whole more than two thirds majority was in favour of abolishing the automatic cost-of-living adjustment, while official declarations from the leaders of the trade unions on the other hand were unanimously against such an intervention. When the government in Denmark later actually did abolish the cost-of-living adjustment, it only gave rise to the usual ritual protests.

However, also within the ethical, economic and legal philosophy of recent years there has been a growing recognition of the need for an economic mechanism ensuring that efficiency, quality and personal liberty play a growing part at the expense of equality. Even *John Rawls,* who in the 1960s formulated a, in principle, Social Democratic moral philosophy based on the principle of equality, and who therefore became the main opponent of *Robert Nozick's* defence of the minimal state, recognized that personal liberty is a value which cannot be reduced to equality or public utility, but has to be a value competing with these. And also the Anglo-American legal philosopher *Ronald Dworkin* has in his later works emphasized that the *commutative* justice and personal liberty must be placed beside the *distributive* justice and equality.[11] I think that this tendency must be preserved and perhaps strengthened, if democracy is to survive: we must let a kind of market mechanism decide essential parts of the distribution of values in society, by means of which the interest in efficiency and equality as well as free choice and personal liberty will be safeguarded at the expense of equality and public utility; however, not to a wider extent than it is compatible with the social and humane morality.

The conception of justice has ever since Aristotle's analysis of it consisted in a *commutative* justice, which dates back to the period before the polity, and which aims at equivalence between performance and payment and between crime and penalty, and a *distributive* justice, which has arisen together with the polity, and which aims at giving every man his due (suum cuique) on the basis of public utility. Also in our time we have to recognize the dialectic relation between these values, which reflects man's double need for *freedom* and *security*.

While Western countries have found it difficult to control modern technology, we have seen how Japan apparently has avoided the above-mentioned »stagflation« reflecting the dilemma of the democracies. Concurrently, to the criminologists' great surprise, Japan has avoided the enormous increase of criminality, which has been a curse in the West in this century.[12]

If I shall try to indicate an explanation, it must roughly be as follows: Until 100 years ago Japan was a closed country, which was completely dominated by collective and objective relations, the family being the principal unit. When at the end of the last century Western technology and the legislation attached to it were introduced into Japan the production was organized in conformity with the collective family ideology, according to which each undertaking is considered as a unit, to which the employees belong, and which, on the other hand, ensures them employment for life. It is self-evident that the employees and the management, who do not regard each other as opponents, have a common interest in securing the survival of the undertaking.

In fact it can be said that the collective (organic) Japanese culture could not produce the technological development, but on the other hand it could control it. Western individualism, which was the conceptual basis of the scientific and technological progress, contains on the other hand some forces, which make it extremely difficult to control society and the undertakings in the present, where the individuals are split up into relations and interests, of which some are those of employers and others those of employees, who organize as opponents and not as persons sharing the responsibility for the interests of the undertakings or of society.

With these indications I shall end my reflections on the crisis of democracy.

Notes

1) See here Skabelse, udvikling og samfund (Creation, Evolution and Society), Acta Jutlandica LX, Samfundsvidenskabelig serie 16, Aarhus Universitet (1985).
2) See to the following especially, Demokratie und Völkerbewegung, Memoria del X Congreso Mundial Ordinario de Filosofía del Derecho y Filosofía Social, vol. II (Mexico 1981) p. 83 ff.

3) See above p. 109 f.

4) *Erik Anners*, Den europeiske rettens historie (1983) p. 218 ff., 323 ff.

5) *Stig Jørgensen*, »Gut« und »Böse« im Wandel der Rechtsauffassung, Ethik und Gerechtigkeit (1980) p. 7 ff.; *same*, Contract as a Form of Life, above p. 129.

6) See *Stig Jørgensen*, »Gut« und »Böse«, l.c. (note 5).

7) Die rechtliche Lage des Menschen in einem ständig wechselnden gesellschaftlichen Modell, in: Österreichische Zeitschrift für Öffentliches Recht (1972) p. 213 ff.

8) See above p. 122 f.

9) See especially *Ole P. Kristensen*, in: Skabelse, udvikling og samfund, l.c. (note 1) p. 227.

10) *Martin Paldam*, Regere eller reagere?, in: Nationaløkonomisk tidsskrift (1980) p. 358 ff.

11) See especially *Ebbe Yndgaard*, in: Skabelse, udvikling og samfund, l.c. (note 1) p. 199.

12) See *Stig Jørgensen*, Pluralis Juris, Acta Jutlandica (1982) p. 24 ff.

13) See *Stig Jørgensen*, Contract as a Form of Life, l.c. (note 5) p. 129.

Previous Publication of the Articles

On Meaning, Opinion and Argumentation, A. Peczenik, J. Uusitalo, Reasoning on Legal Reasoning (1979) p. 87.
Does Reality Exist?, Festschrift für Karl Larenz zum 80. Geburtstag (1983), p. 291.
Basic Norm and Paradox, translation of: Grundnorm und Paradox, Rechtstheorie, Beihaft 5 (1984) p. 179.
The Criteria of Quality, Festschrift für Alois Troller (1986).
Motive and Justification in Legal Decision, abbreviated translation of: Die rechtliche Entscheidung und ihre Begründung, Rhetorische Rechtstheorie, herausgegeben von Ottmar Ballweg und Thomas Michael Seibert (1982) p. 337.
Effectiveness and Morality, Theorie der Normen, Festgabe für Ota Weinberger (1984) p. 119.
What is Law?, (Symposium on Pluralis Juris, Canberra 1985 ...).
Scandinavian Legal Philosophy, Rechtstheorie, Beiheft 9, 1986 p. 289. (Bulletin of the Australian Society of Legal Philosophy, vol. 8 (1984) p. 2.
Pluralis Juris, Archiv für Rechts- und Sozialphilosophie, Beiheft 20 (1984) p. 13.
Private Property, Regulation and Governmental Direction, Objektivierung des Rechtsdenkens, Gedächtnisschrift für Ilmar Tammelo (1984) p. 615.
Contract as a Social Form of Life, Rechtstheorie (1985) Bd. 16. p. 201.
The Crisis of Democracy, Translation of Demokratiets dilemma, Festskrift til Torstein Eckhoff (1986).